OLD TALES AND TALKING

OLD TALES AND TALKING

Quentin Compson in William Faulkner's
Absalom, Absalom! and Related Works

ESTELLA SCHOENBERG

UNIVERSITY PRESS OF MISSISSIPPI
JACKSON
1977

Copyright © 1977 by the
University Press of Mississippi
Manufactured in the United States of America
Printed by Vail-Ballou Press, Inc., Binghamton, New York

Library of Congress Cataloging in Publication Data

Schoenberg, Estella.
  Old tales and talking.

  Includes bibliographical references.
    1. Faulkner, William, 1897–1962. Absalom, Ab-
salom! 2. Faulkner, William, 1897–1962—Characters
—Quentin Compson. I. Title.
PS3511.A86A7   813'.5'2   76-58514
ISBN 0-87805-030-2

This book is for Jack

Item 8: a single sheet ⁴/₅ crossed out. longhand. WF having trouble with the wistaria paragraph:

"*That was the summer before Quentin died: that summer with wistaria everywhere from the spring held on reoccurred, bloomed again: that summer of wistaria in the twilight and his father's cigarsmell and fireflies in soft random in the deep shaggy lawn beneath the veranda. . . .*"

—after 4 false starts, all crossed out, this paragraph copied clean—but without mention of Quentin's death.

—Notes, E. Schoenberg, June 22, 1976, the Jill Faulkner Summers Archive, University of Virginia, Charlottesville.

It was a summer of wistaria. The twilight was full of it and of the smell of his father's cigar as they sat on the front gallery after supper until it would be time for Quentin to start, while in the deep shaggy lawn below the veranda the fireflies blew and drifted in soft random. . . .

—*Absalom, Absalom!*, Random House, 1936 the beginning of Chapter II.

Contents

Acknowledgments

I am grateful to many people and several institutions for assistance and support in the preparation of this book, especially to Mrs. Jill Faulkner Summers for allowing me to examine the manuscripts of "Evangeline" and other items in her archive at the University of Virginia, to Dr. James W. Webb of the University of Mississippi and the late Linton B. Massey for encouragement and information as well as their time and courtesy, and to Dr. James G. Watson of the University of Tulsa for seeing me through the initial study on which this book is based.

The libraries of the University of Tulsa and the University of Mississippi have been helpful, but the Manuscript Collection of the University of Virginia, Linton Massey's Faulkner Collection, and the Jill Faulkner Summers Archive—all in the Alderman Library in Charlottesville—have been invaluable. There I found the substantive proof (detailed in my Chapters II, III, and IV) that I had drawn the right conclusions (Chapters V, VI, and VII) from my reading of *Absalom, Absalom!*.

This study would have been difficult without the broad base provided by other scholars in a truly awesome and growing bibliography of Faulkner studies. Editors of essay collections in book form or in special editions of periodicals occasionally gather the best and offer it in manageable parcels. Biblio-graphic studies (for example, James B. Meriwether's "The Short Fiction of William Faulkner: A Bibliography" in *PROOF: The Yearbook of American Bibliographical and Textual Studies*, Vol. I, ed. Joseph Katz, 1971) provide a sturdy framework for investigative reading.

Joseph Blotner's *Faulkner: A Biography* (Random House, 1974) was published after I was well into this study. It fills a long-standing need for what is called a full-scale account of Faulkner's life and career. The two volumes have been useful to me, as they will be to all who are curious about William Faulkner and his books.

Publication of Faulkner's correspondence was begun in 1966 with The *Faulkner-Cowley File* (Random House). To that volume edited by Malcolm Cowley, which includes Cowley's as well as Faulkner's letters, Dr. Blotner has now added *Selected Letters of William Faulkner* (Random House, 1977).

The Sutpen chronology in *Absalom, Absalom!* has been the subject of continuing exchanges among scholars since the publication of the novel in 1936. Rather than extend the debate along lines established by precedent, I have chosen not to challenge by careful citation each attempt at what I believe a futile endeavor. This kind of intellectual in-fighting serves no purpose but that of scholarly one-upmanship. For the most part I have identified the authors of given points only to agree with them. Without exception the wrong guesses (as I see them) also have been made by men and women of good faith, most of them sound scholars, and I see no reason to name those authors only to say that they were wrong or misguided. If I am lucky, others will deal as gently or as circumspectly with my misjudgments.

Acknowledgments

However, if any of my readers want to trace the chronological controversy, I would refer them to John Hagopian, "Black Insight in *Absalom, Absalom!*." This paper was read in Buffalo, New York, October 9, 1975. It concerns the source of Quentin's information that Charles Bon was part Negro. In his paper, Professor Hagopian refers to almost all important scholarship on *Absalom, Absalom!* since 1962, especially as it addresses the question of Bon's parentage. When he read the paper to the Northern New York College English Association, the author announced that an expanded version was to be published in *Studies in Twentieth Century Literature.*

OLD TALES AND TALKING

Introduction

In the early pages of *Absalom, Absalom!* Quentin Compson asks himself, and then asks his father, why Rosa Coldfield has chosen him to write the story of Thomas Sutpen. Mr. Compson's explanation, that Quentin is a descendant of Sutpen's friend, General Jason Compson, CSA, is not really satisfactory to Quentin. The reader has even better grounds for the same question once removed—why did William Faulkner choose to tell Sutpen's story through Quentin—and why is the telling done during Quentin's freshman year at Harvard, his last year of life?

These questions stir up other problems, issues fundamental to the most primitive and the most sophisticated processes of fiction—invention and narration—and the relationships, a triple bond, of the teller, the tale, and the listener.

A close look at *Absalom, Absalom!* reveals Quentin in all three of these parts. He is first the listener and then the teller, and throughout the book he is his creator's subject: a despairing youth confronted with a collection of "old ghost tales."

The character of Quentin Compson, the events of his life from infancy to suicide, his relationships with the members of his family, and his feelings about the tradition into which he has been born, all these were established in an earlier novel, *The Sound and the Fury*, yet Faulkner does not refer in *Absalom, Absalom!* to even the most pertinent of them—Quentin's distress over his sister Caddy and then his suicide. Neither does he alter the characters or the chronology of *The Sound and the Fury* in this narrative, through Quentin, of what most readers have considered the primary story of *Absalom, Absalom!*, the story of Thomas Sutpen and his children.

But Sutpen's is not unquestionably the primary story. It is at least as easy—for me much easier—to see the story of Quentin Compson in the foreground of *Absalom, Absalom!* and to hear in the book's title Jason Richmond Compson's grief for his son Quentin. Quentin's handling of the Sutpen material is, from this viewpoint, a demonstration or case history of the process through which any piece of fiction is developed by its author from a few "facts" and (more important) a few mental pictures. Quentin's working out the story of Sutpen's children in this novel is Faulkner's means of retelling Quentin's story and explaining Quentin's suicide.

In many ways *Absalom, Absalom!* is a central microfiction within the macrofiction of Yoknapatawpha County or—a somewhat wider field—the complete fiction of William Faulkner, or beyond that the twentieth-century American novel, or beyond that . . . the ripples seem unending.

Quentin's suicide is not mentioned in *Absalom, Absalom!*, but unless the reader knows of it Quentin's dejection and psychic withdrawal throughout the last half of the novel are not adequately explained. Although the information is crucial to understanding of *Absalom, Absalom!*, Faulkner's readers must bring with them from *The Sound and the Fury* on their own initiative their own knowledge that Quentin in his fresh-

man year at Harvard is distraught because his sister Caddy
has dishonored herself and her family, that he has failed effectively to control the situation or his grief, and that he will end
his life (has already ended it in the earlier novel) at the end of
the school year by plunging into the Charles River in Cambridge.

Against this too easily unnoticed background Quentin is
engaged throughout *Absalom, Absalom!* with the legends of
Sutpen, stories he has known all his life. On command he re-
tells them, but in the retelling he elaborates them, extends
them, and deliberately distorts them. To explain Quentin's
contributions to these old tales is to explain at least some of
the elements of the process of fictionalizing as a professional
fictionalist—William Faulkner—understood them; and since
fiction and reality are so easily confused under the best and
clearest conditions, it may be to explain or seem to explain
Quentin's (and Faulkner's) understanding of the difference or
sameness of "be" and "seems," "was" and "must have been."

Why does a writer or teller of tales tell it as he does tell it?
Where does he get his plot and why does that plot turn this
way and not that at its climax? We cannot help wondering,
but we should be cautious, because the next question is Why
does the critic think what *he* thinks? Where does *he* find the
explanation of the writer's design?

In *Absalom, Absalom!* Faulkner has provided a buffered
zone for our exploration—not just Quentin the fictionalist but
Quentin's half-dozen or more informants and their sources
beyond them. Faulkner attributes to Quentin the novel's controlling image of ripples spreading in water:

"Yes," Quentin said. "The two children" thinking *Yes. Maybe we
are both Father. Maybe nothing ever happens once and is fin-*

ished. Maybe happen is never once but like ripples maybe on water after the pebble sinks, the ripples moving on, spreading, the pool attached by a narrow umbilical water-cord to the next pool which the first pool feeds, has fed, did feed, let this second pool contain a different temperature of water, a different molecularity of having seen, felt, remembered, reflect in a different tone the infinite unchanging sky, it doesn't matter: that pebble's watery echo whose fall it did not even see moves across its surface too and the original ripple-space, to the old ineradicable rhythm thinking Yes, we are both Father. *Or maybe Father and I are both Shreve, maybe it took Father and me both to make Shreve or Shreve and me both to make Father or maybe Thomas Sutpen to make all of us.* (AA, 161–62) [1]

---

[1] Page references to *Absalom, Absalom!* and *The Sound and the Fury* will be in parentheses with the abbreviations *AA* and *SF*. There is bound to be some confusion about the form of quotations from both these novels. Faulkner used italics, for instance, to indicate other things than the usual vocal emphasis. Frequently his italics signal a change in point of view or a shift from a character's "present" actions and conversation to his memory or to present internal monologue. Wherever quotations from Faulkner's works are used in this book, italics and quotation marks are as they appear in his text. Editions cited are Vintage Books (Random House), which preserve the pagination of the first editions: *The Sound and the Fury*, 1929, and *Absalom, Absalom!*, 1936.

I
A Novel inside a Novel:
The Quentin Chronology

"Never once but like ripples" is a good way to represent the
echo effect of characterizations, incidents, and situations
Faulkner moved from *The Sound and the Fury* to *Absalom,
Absalom!* Ellen Sutpen, for instance, is an avatar (Faulkner's
word) of Caroline Compson in her engineering (Mr. Compson's word) her daughter's engagement, her inability to understand or help husband or children, and her fluttery descent into illness. The child Charles Etienne Saint-Valery Bon
and his situation are much the same as Caddy's daughter
Quentin and her situation: for each there is questionable legit-
imacy unsuccessfully established by the mother's spurious
marriage; each is brought, out of love for the child's "lost"
parent, to be reared in a house where the child finds neither
love nor comfort and very little physical ease; each child has
its nose rubbed in the transgressions of its parents until the
child rebels against its "benevolent" oppressor and against the
world, rushing into an alliance which proclaims not self-
indulgence but self-debasement for the sole seeming purpose
of punishing everyone and rewarding no one.

These are only two of many examples. The "ripples" or re-
currences are of two kinds: those that stop Quentin dead in
his tracks because they are so like his own experience, and

those recognizable only to the reader because they reenact parts of *The Sound and the Fury* which occur after January 1910, when Quentin tells Shreve about the Sutpens—some even recalling events which followed, by months or years, Quentin's suicide.

Of Quentin's family in *The Sound and the Fury*, only he and his father appear in *Absalom, Absalom!* The rest of the Compsons have vanished between novels, taking their house itself, except for the front porch, and their servants with them. But in both novels Quentin has long serious talks with his father and carries his father's words always in his mind, and in both novels he departs in September 1909 from Jefferson for his freshman year at Harvard.

In late summer, 1909, Caddy (in *The Sound and the Fury*) surrenders her virginity to Dalton Ames. Quentin, beside himself, offers to run away with Caddy, to commit incest with her or take the blame for it, to kill both Caddy and himself. He confronts Ames and comes off second best. He tries unsuccessfully to convince his father that he and Caddy have committed incest and then that he will kill himself. Quentin's father urges him, during their twilight talk on the gallery, to leave early for Harvard and spend a month in Maine.

Evidently Quentin did not leave early, for at the beginning of September 1909 (in *Absalom, Absalom!*) he is still at home when Miss Rosa Coldfield involves him in the Sutpen story. Quentin has "always" known about Sutpen and his daughter whose brother killed her fiance making her a widow before she was a bride. He learns more now from Rosa and from his father. Mr. Compson also gives Quentin an "artifact"—a letter Charles Bon is said to have written to Judith Sutpen in 1865.

8

Quentin and his father talk at length about the nature of incest (in both novels). After dark that same evening, Quentin accompanies Miss Rosa out to Sutpen's Hundred where he comes face to face with Henry Sutpen, now old and dying. The next day Quentin leaves for Harvard.

In December, returning to Mississippi for the Christmas holidays (*The Sound and the Fury*), Quentin tosses a quarter to a Negro during a brief train stop in Virginia and promises to come that way again two days after the New Year. This schedule means he was at home when Rosa took an ambulance out to the old Sutpen house to bring Henry in to town; he would have known about the fire which destroyed the crumbling mansion with Henry and his mulatto half-sister Clytie in it and about Rosa's collapse.

Indeed, Mr. Compson's letter to Quentin (*Absalom, Absalom!*), mailed on January 10, implies that Quentin did know Rosa was dying. The letter reports her death without mention of the fire and describes her funeral. It also contains remarks on death and the experience of dying which take on added significance in light of Quentin's suicide threats (*The Sound and the Fury*) at the end of the preceding summer.

Mr. Compson's letter is the occasion of Quentin's long talk with his Canadian roommate, Shreve McCannon, about the Sutpens. As the roommates reconstruct the story of Henry and Charles and Judith, it does not turn out as Caddy's story turns out in *The Sound and the Fury*; in January Quentin has still to learn of Caddy's engagement to Sidney Herbert Head and of her pregnancy. The long narrative session in the cold dormitory room culminates in Quentin's denial that he hates the South. This is the end of *Absalom, Absalom!*

In April 1910 Quentin goes home for Caddy's wedding and

has to be told that she is pregnant. He promises Caddy he will assume full responsibility for their father and for their idiot brother Benjy. After the wedding Quentin returns to Harvard and finishes the school year.

On June 2, 1910, Quentin commits suicide by drowning in the Charles River. The day of his death is detailed in the second section of *The Sound and the Fury*. The only specific reference to it in *Absalom, Absalom!* is at the end of the genealogy appended to the novel, where Quentin's date of death is noted, 1910, as simply as his date of birth, 1891.

In November 1910 Caddy's daughter is born (unless she was born prematurely) and named for her uncle, Quentin. Caddy's husband casts her off, and Mr. Compson brings the baby to be reared in Jefferson. He has been drinking heavily, as Caddy and Quentin were aware, and about a year after the birth of his granddaughter Quentin and eighteen months after the death of his son Quentin, Mr. Compson dies.

No allowances are necessary, and no adjustments, to show that September 1909 in *Absalom, Absalom!* follows, in the normal flow of chronological sequence, August 1909 in *The Sound and the Fury*, or to prove that Quentin's insight into the story Rosa Coldfield thrusts upon him in September is made not only possible but inescapable by what he has been through in August with Caddy and Dalton Ames.

For similar reasons, Quentin's father sees Ellen Sutpen as much like his wife, Caroline, and it is he who gives Faulkner's readers a picture of the child Rosa Coldfield that displays the same sympathetic understanding of individual children that characterized Mr. Compson in *The Sound and the Fury*.

Also for similar reasons, Rosa's account of Sutpen history is a firsthand account in a very limited sense. She participated in that history, but long ago, and her account of it is almost as fictionalized as Quentin's and Shreve's. Like Quentin's, it is shaped by emotions and faulty memory. As Rosa says herself, "the resultant sum" of such remembering "is usually incorrect and false and worthy only of the name of dream." Even Shreve, who has no memory of the South or knowledge of Southerners, in his eagerness to join the story-telling game contributes insightful conclusions about Charles Bon and Henry which reveal the same slightly bemused, slightly dense, gruff-but-good-natured supportive attitude with which he stands by Quentin in *The Sound and the Fury*.

It is probably safe to say, even in words of one syllable, that this is how all bards work and how all tales take shape. Logically extending this conclusion, if Faulkner knew he was saying through Quentin in *Absalom, Absalom!* that the author's experience shapes and limits his invention, he must have anticipated someone sometime looking for the writer William Faulkner behind his narrator Quentin Compson behind their subject Henry Sutpen. I have tried to hold my investigation of *Absalom, Absalom!* back from biographical interpretation of Faulkner—except as an inventor of fiction. My main concerns are Quentin, his double function as protagonist and narrator in *Absalom, Absalom!*, and what that double function reveals about the fictive process.

I should like to have been able to explain the peculiar strategy by which Faulkner kept out of *Absalom, Absalom!* all reference to Caddy, the other characters, and all the events of *The Sound and the Fury*. Their absence forces too heavy reliance on awareness of the earlier novel. Unless the reader has recently experienced that novel and has it firmly in mind, the cost is too great. Perhaps Faulkner felt that his choice of Quentin as primary narrator had so enriched and so complicated *Absalom, Absalom!* that he could hardly afford to explicate his own narrative technique for fear of over-complexity. The alternative is over-subtlety—irony.

There is, of course, a third possibility—that Faulkner, who was notorious for his stubborn defense of an author's right to privacy, was so keenly aware of his identification with Quentin's role of story-teller, where he lays bare for astute readers the secrets of his ancient trade and might seem to imply further parallels with his own, Quentin's creator's, life, that he did not wish to spell out the foundations of Quentin's fabrications even by reference to an earlier fiction. He just did not want to bring up the issue.

But the novel is, after all, about the process of Quentin's hearing and developing stories. Even critics who emphasize the substance of the Sutpen legends over their telling recognize this narrative device in *Absalom, Absalom!* Furthermore, the most important facts about Quentin are not autobiographical. Faulkner had no sister at all, and he did not commit suicide.

After the birth of Faulkner's first daughter, who lived only a few days, and before the birth of his daughter Jill, he wrote that perhaps he had invented little Caddy to be the daughter he had been denied. But Caddy is Quentin's sister. That the author, who had three brothers, might have wished for a sister or at least have wondered what it would be like to have one is suggested by the frequency of strong brother-sister pairing of characters in his early works. None of Faulkner's pairs, however, not even Narcissa and Horace Benbow in *Sartoris (Flags in the Dust)*, are as close or as mutually destructive as Caddy and Quentin Compson.

The brother-sister contrast or complement, as a matter of

simple narrative craftsmanship, is one of the easiest and oldest means of establishing character and conflict in a plot. It has been used in poetry, legend, and drama as long as anyone knows about those literary forms.

On the second point—that Faulkner did not commit suicide—I would touch very gingerly. For one thing, I am not a professional psychologist, much less a psychoanalyst, and for another thing, it seems to me improbable if not impossible that a dead man's psyche can be accurately reconstructed from the ragtag and bob-ends of even the most heavily documented biographies and memories—as Faulkner himself demonstrated in Quentin's search for the Sutpen past. It is enough to the point that Quentin's suicidal despair is extraordinarily well-imagined, and that generally acknowledged alternatives to the irreversible plunge into oblivion include alcohol and the creative imagination, both of which Faulkner knew well.[1]

---

[1] A recent extreme example of psychological and biographical inquiry into literature focuses on precisely the subjects of this book, William Faulkner and his novel *Absalom, Absalom!*: John T. Irwin, *Doubling and Incest/Repetition and Revenge: A Speculative Reading of Faulkner* (The Johns Hopkins University Press, 1975).

Basing his inquiry on an admittedly unprofessional but enthusiastic acquaintance with the writings of Sigmund Freud and ignoring any developments in psychology since Freud, Professor Irwin probes the psyches of various fictional characters including Charles Bon, Henry Sutpen, and Quentin Compson, and also the psyche of their no-longer-available creator, William Faulkner. Offering them as representative of all men fictional and real, he arrives at the conclusion that art is a means of self-indulgence and self-gratification—a kind of ultimate incest, the enactment of self-love.

Irwin's own ultimate self-indulgence in this book consists of an attempt, honorable enough in art but impractical in criticism and analysis of art, to devise a style and a structure appropriate to its basic statement. Unlike Faulkner, who gambled like a true Southerner that his readers would discern what he was up to without having to be told, Irwin carefully describes

Objectivity demands recognition of the fact that Quentin is only one of many fictional characters created by William Faulkner over a long and productive career. Quentin cannot possibly be more Faulkner than he is Quentin Compson, and Faulkner could not have been more Quentin than he was himself or there would have been no *Absalom, Absalom!* for us to analyze or to enjoy.

For the most part I have been able to resist too close scru-

---

his intent to say everything simultaneously throughout the book but to withhold resolution of each point until the last possible page, there to focus it all and state it all, again simultaneously.

Irwin arrives at some of the same conclusions to be found in this study of Quentin Compson and the fictive process. He was, after all, dealing with the same material and asking essentially the same questions. But where he relies too heavily on application of Freudian "classic" situations to Quentin's and Faulkner's problems, it seems to me he misconstrues or ignores the evidence. For instance, I believe Irwin misunderstands the relationship of Quentin and his father and tries to make Quentin's problems fit the Oedipus pattern too precisely. Mr. Compson's humanity and his concerned love for his son have no part in Irwin's characterization of him as a man who fails to read his son's signals for help and for that reason fails to act effectively for Quentin's salvation.

In discussing *Mosquitoes*, Faulkner's second novel, late in his own book, Irwin draws important conclusions from the convictions and ideas of characters in that novel, conclusions about the substitutional or sublimational value of creative activity. He does not qualify these convictions as those of fictional characters, nor does he suggest that whether or not a character speaks the conviction of the author, the character's opinion or belief is supplied him by the author as a part of his persona, the part he is required to act, or that without it the plot would grind to a halt—that there are pragmatic considerations to the building of a novel.

I would argue with Irwin that he has stacked his cards without acknowledging that novelists do the same thing. I would not try to prove him wrong on every point, or even totally wrong on his most important points, but I would like to convince him that a fictionalist is good, better, or best in relation to his ability vividly to create even unsympathetic characters, that *all* his characters speak for aspects of the author's self, and that not all problems are psychological or masculine or artistic.

tiny of the biographic ripple, but my restraint does not compare with the restraint by which Faulkner avoided in *Absalom, Absalom!* reference to Quentin's biography as presented in *The Sound and the Fury.*

The author's dependence on irony in *Absalom, Absalom!* has unjustly limited for forty years the emotional and intellectual experience of his readers. Either he overestimated their ability to recognize irony or he underestimated their capacity for richness. Even without recognition of this outer dimension, though, *Absalom, Absalom!* has been judged very highly. Many critics consider it Faulkner's masterpiece. Of greater importance than its excellence, though, are this novel's many statements about the nature and processes of fiction and the creation of fiction.

II

Continuums within Continuums:
Quentin Compson

Faulkner used both the Sutpen material and Quentin Compson in fictions before and after *Absalom, Absalom!*, but that novel is his only explicit combination of the two. Their interaction there must account for the richness of texture, the vitality, and ultimately the success of *Absalom, Absalom!*—for the Sutpen material failed in every other use. As for Quentin, Faulkner continued to employ him, especially as a narrator, even after Quentin's suicide, although in these "posthumous" performances Quentin's identity had to be masked and his name either changed or dropped, and his importance to the story had to be diminished—usually restricted to the narrative frame.

The history of Quentin's childhood and his apprenticeship to the narrative craft is well established in two published stories long recognized as preliminary to *The Sound and the Fury*—"That Evening Sun Go Down" (later titled simply "That Evening Sun") [1] and "A Justice." [2]

In these two stories Quentin's family ties are described es-

---

[1] "That Evening Sun Go Down," *American Mercury*, XXII (March 1931); "That Evening Sun" in *These 13* (Cape and Smith, 1931) and in *Collected Stories of William Faulkner* (Random House, 1950).
[2] "A Justice" in *These 13* and in *Collected Stories*.

sentially as they stand in *The Sound and the Fury*—except that Benjy is missing. Quentin's mother is a distant disappointment, his father a gentle, faintly inadequate comfort, and there are two younger children, Caddy and Jason. A child in these stories, Quentin observes and listens to adults and stores up memories of experience to be understood (and written) when he will have grown up himself.

In "That Evening Sun Go Down" Quentin, Caddy, and Jason are exposed to the growing hysteria of Nancy, a Negro woman who believes her estranged husband will murder her. Only Quentin, the oldest child, is aware at all that something awesome is happening. In this story Quentin's father is in charge not only of adult household affairs but also of the children, with whom he is firm but gentle—a calm and (to them) reassuring presence.

(Faulkner's ambiguity at the end of "That Evening Sun" led to considerable confusion as to whether Jesus, the husband, really was lurking nearby and really did kill Nancy. Adding to the confusion, a seeming misprint—Nancy for Fancy—in *The Sound and the Fury* puts Nancy's bones rather than the bones of the pony Fancy in a ditch for the Compson children to fear and marvel at; but the bones of not even a Negro woman, not even in Mississippi, not even at the turn of the century, would have been left to bleach in the open.)

In "A Justice" Caddy and Jason are again with Quentin, but instead of their father Grandfather Compson is there driving the children in his buggy out to the farm, where Caddy muddies her drawers in the creek while Quentin listens to Sam Fathers tell how he came to be named Fathers, or Two Fathers—another story Quentin realizes he will not understand fully until he is older.

Quentin is named in only one other published short story, an early version of Faulkner's more than twice told tale of a boy's (here Quentin's, later Ike McCaslin's) initiation by Sam Fathers to the hunt. The story, named "Lion" for the great hunting dog familiar to readers of "The Bear" and *Go Down, Moses,* was published in 1935,[3] but its characterization of Quentin suggests a much earlier writing. In fact, all three of the stories belong to a time before Faulkner had begun to think of Quentin as a suicide or had added Benjy to the Compson family for the incorruptible innocence of Benjy's idiocy.

In all these stories the Quentin who recalls incidents of his childhood has outlived the Quentin who plunged into the Charles River to end his life before he was twenty-one. A little simple arithmetic with the children's ages and the number of years "since then" makes the adult narrator of "A Justice" twenty-six.

In three other short stories Faulkner again employed a narrative frame structure, but perhaps because these stories were published after *The Sound and the Fury* and because their observer-narrator is so objective and apparently healthy in his outlook, Quentin's name does not appear—although details of one kind or another point to his identity. The stories are "The Old People," "A Bear Hunt," and "Fool About a Horse." [4] The first two, hunting stories, found their way into *Go Down,*

[3] *Harper's,* CLXXII (December 1935).
[4] "The Old People," *Harper's,* CLXXXI (September 1940) and, revised, in *Go Down, Moses* (Random House, 1942) and *Big Woods* (Random House, 1955); "A Bear Hunt," *Saturday Evening Post,* CCVI (February 10, 1934), also in *Collected Stories* and *Big Woods;* "Fool About a Horse," *Scribner's,* C (August 1936).

Moses and *Big Woods*. The third, a tall tale of horse trading, was used, with a new cast of characters, to open *The Hamlet*, the first novel of the Snopes trilogy.

Quentin is easy to identify in "The Old People," where the adult first-person narrator recalls his initiation to the hunt, very similar to the story "Lion." Again the initiation is conducted by Sam Fathers. Again the boy's father is present (Ike McCaslin might have some claim to this story, but Ike had no father to advise and encourage him), and again there are references to "our farm" and "Father's office." There is also a deliberate reference to "A Justice," a story set, like this one, when the boy was twelve: "Sam told me about that."

V. K. Suratt (later V. K. Ratliff) is the primary narrator of "Fool About a Horse" and "A Bear Hunt." The itinerant sewing machine salesman was one of Faulkner's favorite characters, an entertaining information monger and plot catalyst; but in both these stories the telling is set up for Suratt by a frame narrator who is the same adult remembering childhood who related the story of "The Old People."

In a frame which Faulkner deleted when he revised "Fool About a Horse" for *The Hamlet*, V. K. Suratt spins his yarn in a lawyer's office overlooking Jefferson's town square. The boy who as a grown man introduces the story as Suratt's was present at the telling with several of his elders. The boy might almost be Chick Mallison and the law office his uncle's, but the adult listeners include the boy's grandfather and Doc Peabody, the Compson family physician (also intimate with Chick and his family, of course), and Roskus, the Compson's Negro servant, Dilsey's husband, who hands around the bourbon and water.

In "A Bear Hunt" the adult narrator describes himself at fifteen as belonging to a "literate, town-bred family." The frame of this story is much more elaborate and contains its own complete story which offsets and frames another rowdy tale of the hunting camp—the story of how Lucius Provine's hiccups were cured by means of a practical joke. In the frame, however, the story is serious. In it the boy's attitude toward Indians, Negroes, cruelty, and the land, as well as references to his home and family, echo or duplicate the attitude of Quentin as it has been established in other stories—concerned, sensitive, perceptive within the limits of his maturity, and willing to wait for further maturity to reveal to him the full meaning of what he observes and stores for future narration.

The story of Provine's hiccups was written after a hunting trip in 1933 during which Faulkner himself suffered an attack of the hiccups. The frame story, very different in tone, was not necessarily invented at the same time.

In 1925 William Faulkner sailed from New Orleans, landed eventually at Genoa, and walked northward through Italy and Switzerland with his friend William Spratling. Spratling, an architect and artist, sketched his way along the route while Faulkner talked and wrote—prolifically in both modes, Spratling told Joseph Blotner.

The travelers had adventures of their own, of course, but Faulkner wrote at least four stories (their dates of composition are not known) employing the collaborative narration of two travelers, unquestionably patterned on himself and Spratling, who walk along the same route he and Spratling followed and apply their creative imaginations to the building of stories

from the situations and people they encounter. In each case
they believe themselves to be calculating truth, but in no case
does Faulkner "admit" to the reader that their conclusions are
correct.

The fictional narrators are Don and his unnamed friend, the
narrator—"I." As he began the writing of *Absalom, Absalom!*
Faulkner moved these two narrators through at least two
metamorphoses. For a while they were, as in the stories, Don
and I. Then they were Chisholm and Burke. At one point,
briefly, they seem to have been combined as contrasting sides
of a single mind—Quentin's. In the end they became Quentin
and Shreve—or maybe they had been Quentin and his friend
all along. Don's friend could easily be the same Quentin who
wrote "A Justice" at the age of twenty-six.

The Don-and-I stories are "Mistral," "The Big Shot,"
"Snow," and "Evangeline." [5] Of these only "Mistral" achieved
publication, but "Snow" and "The Big Shot" have been
known for some time.

[5] "Mistral," *These 13* and *Collected Stories.* The Manuscript Collection at
the University of Virginia includes carbon typescripts of "Mistral," "Snow,"
and "The Big Shot." The last two, and other unpublished Faulkner material,
are described in the *Mississippi Quarterly: Special Issue, William Faulkner,*
XXVI, 3 (Summer 1973). See also Joseph Blotner, *Faulkner: A Biography*
(Random House, 1974), 2 vols.

"Evangeline" has been presented only by Blotner (*ibid.*). My assertions
about the Don-and-I narrators in this chapter and my recapitulations of their
four stories in the next chapter are founded on my examination of the
typescripts of all four stories as well as "Mistral" as published and a manuscript of "Evangeline" which is a shorter draft of the typescript. The manuscript and typescript of "Evangeline" are among the papers of the Jill
Faulkner Summers Archive, as are several false starts on the novel *Absalom,
Absalom!*

The papers of this archive, some 2,000 pages of manuscript and type-

Although Don's unnamed friend introduces each of the four
stories, he does so as briefly as possible and then hands the
telling around among Don and himself and the people they
talk with either singly or together. In each story the narrator
identifies himself and Don, slightly varying their professions
from story to story, and sets the time of the "present" telling
in relation to the time of the story being told. Most of the
frames seem to have been adjusted with regard to time to
make the telling approximately contemporary with the time
Faulkner submitted the stories for publication.

In "Mistral" the travelers are in Italy. In "Snow," a similar
story, they have progressed to Switzerland, but the frame of
"Snow" is set fifteen years later, during World War II. Here
the updating is more obvious, for the frame's relation to the
primary story is almost embarrassingly artificial.

In "The Big Shot" Don and his friend are back in the American South, before World War II, probably during Prohibi-
tion. The introduction is brief and matter-of-fact, but Don's
last name is given in "The Big Shot"—the only time it is mentioned in any of the stories. He is Don Reeves and he has
been a reporter for the Memphis *Sentinel*. (Very little pho-
netic maneuvering is required to transform Reeves to Shreve,
or vice versa.)

---

script, were found at the Faulkner home, Rowan Oak, in Oxford, Mississippi, in August 1971. The collection will be referred to hereafter as either
the Jill Faulkner Summers Archive or the Rowan Oak papers.

The find was reported in syndicated news stories early in 1972. *The New
York Times*, for instance: "Faulkner Papers Are Found At His Mississippi
Home," datelined Oxford, Miss., Jan. 9 (AP), page 29—a three-inch item.
The Arkansas Gazette (Little Rock) used a 14½-inch account by Reuters
seven weeks later: "Manuscripts of Faulkner Are Discovered," *The Gazette*,
Sun., Feb. 27, 1972, page 22A.

In "Evangeline" Don is an architect who has been sketching the façades of antebellum houses in northern Mississippi. His friend identifies himself in this story as the reporter, "a writer, a man that writes pieces for newspapers, and such." The date of both the frame and the primary story of "Evangeline" is seven years after the narrator's last meeting with Don, presumably seven years after their travels in Europe.

If any of the Don-and-I stories was written when its frame indicates it was, it would be this one. For one thing, the setting of both frame and story is the same. For another thing, the writing here is more polished, the style more sophisticated and elaborate, than in any of the other tales. In contrast to this earliest known writing of "Evangeline" the other Don-and-I stories are almost Hemingway-like in the brevity and directness of their sentences and in the handling of foreign languages by suggestion.

The draft, however, has very few miss-licks. It could represent the reworking of earlier material—material always, even in *Absalom, Absalom!*, too miscellaneous for complete resolution.

To follow the Quentin narrator, the young writer who seems to be the friend and traveling companion of a young architect-artist or journalist named Don, it is necessary to ignore Quentin the suicide. In *The Sound and the Fury*, in fact, Quentin demonstrates no narrative skill or inclination at all. Story-telling has been a part of his life, as shown by his fond memory of Louis Hatcher's voice telling ridiculous stories about the Mississippi aftermath of the Johnstown flood, but Quentin as a fictionalist is completely unsuccessful in the novel in which he ends his own life. He cannot convince anyone of anything, whether he is trying to tell the truth or to lie. The stream-of-consciousness technique Faulkner chose for Quentin's section of the novel is as far removed from narrative by Quentin as it can possibly be, although as a narrative device for Faulkner himself it is very powerful indeed.

In *Absalom, Absalom!* the two Quentins—narrator and suicide—are of almost equal importance, then the balance tips again toward the narrator.

Any fictional character, but especially one whose basic function is narrative, embodies important aspects of his own creator, also a teller of tales. To propose that Quentin Compson the fictionalist is fundamentally a persona of William Faulkner the fictionalist is not, however, to insist that the details of Quentin's life are autobiographical on Faulkner's part. He and Quentin shared a great deal, most importantly the setting of their childhoods, the legends of Mississippi, and the profession of writing. I do not wish to claim that Quentin *was* Faulkner or that Faulkner *was* Quentin, but that there was a great deal of each in the mind style of the other. This was, after all, under the control of William Faulkner, who depended heavily on intermediaries to his own narrative voice.

The line between deliberate and unintentional in the building of fiction is by its very nature blurred; but there *is* a distinction, and a professional writer never (well, hardly ever) puts on paper less than he means to—or a great deal more.

However, by the time Faulkner was asked to write a major magazine piece on Mississippi for *Holiday* magazine, he was ready to do it in a kind of personalized third-person, referring obviously to himself as "he," "the boy," "the young man," and then "the middle-aged." [6]

[6] William Faulkner, "Mississippi," *Holiday*, XV (April 1954), 33–47.

In the magazine article, this strange first/third person essay-ist reports as his own a mixture of memories belonging partly to William Faulkner and partly to Quentin Compson. Most striking of all, he states his ambivalence of love and hate for the South in near quotations from *Absalom, Absalom!*

Faulkner's last novel, *The Reivers* (Random House, 1962), is about a boy, Lucius Priest. The boy has a grandfather, Grandfather Priest, from whom he learns a great deal and from whom he and Boon Hogganbeck steal or borrow Jeffer-son's second automobile (the one owned in the history of Oxford, Mississippi, by Faulkner's grandfather) for a trouble-fraught joy-ride to Memphis. The story is told as a reminis-cence by Lucius, himself now Grandfather Priest, to his grandsons. The light-hearted comedy of human error is brought to a moral conclusion for their edification.

After a lifetime of writing about the tangled relationships of Yoknapatawpha County's inhabitants, Faulkner here in-troduces a family completely new to his readers, a family sup-posedly well-established and long resident in the county and the town. The story involves Boon Hogganbeck and other fa-miliar names and faces, but Lucius and the other Priests are, like the narrator of "Mississippi," a complex of autobio-graphical and fictional characters by William Faulkner.

Lucius Priest, the grandfather, is easy to identify with Wil-liam Faulkner, the grandfather who dedicated *The Reivers* to his daughter's little boys. Lucius, the boy, is in many respects the most Quentin-like of all Faulkner's protagonist-narrators.

Lucius-Quentin is, in the first place, a gentleman. He has learned from his father and his grandfather that there are some things a gentleman always does and some things a gen-tleman never does. He learns in a Memphis brothel what

Quentin learned through Caddy, but his story is warm and comic where Quentin's own (in *The Sound and the Fury* and *Absalom, Absalom!*) was tragic; but the greatest difference between the two boys is in their reactions to the loss of innocence. This difference may be explainable in terms of Faulkner's age at the time he wrote each of their stories. The Quentin who commits suicide over his sister's loss of virtue and his own agony of incestuous love was created by a comparatively young and basically romantic fictionalist who had newly perfected the difficult arts of prose fiction. Young Lucius Priest, whose grandfather convinces him that he can "live with" his comparatively minor shame, is the fond creation of a mature humanist who improvises freely with the inventive and narrative skills in which he has long delighted.

At the beginning of *Absalom, Absalom!* Quentin feels that there are two of him—one preparing to leave Jefferson for a year at Harvard University, the other being forced into the job of local historian and raconteur. Reluctantly but compulsively he plunges into the legends of Sutpen, rehearsing them even while hearing them, one of the Quentins collaborating with the other:

> *It seems that this demon—his name was Sutpen—(Colonel Sutpen)—Colonel Sutpen. Who came out of nowhere and without warning upon the land with a band of strange niggers and built a plantation—(Tore violently a plantation, Miss Rosa Coldfield says)—tore violently. And married her sister Ellen and begot a son and a daughter which (Without gentleness begot, Miss Rosa Coldfield says)—without gentleness. Which should have been the jewels of his pride and the shield and comfort of his old age, only—(Only they destroyed him or something or he destroyed*

26

them or something. And died)—and died. Without regret, Miss
Rosa Coldfield says—(Save by her) Yes, save by her. (And by
Quentin Compson) Yes. And by Quentin Compson. (AA, 9)

Recruited by Rosa Coldfield to his narrative responsibility,
Quentin is helpless to resist for two reasons: first, he is a
polite young man easily drafted to the service of a little old
lady poet; and second, he sees in the stories of Judith and
Henry Sutpen a situation with which he is personally familiar
but which he has been unable to resolve. In Sutpen terms it
is the Henry-Judith-Charles Bon triangle. In Quentin's terms
the triangle binds Quentin to Caddy to Dalton Ames.

The coinciding triangles are to have their acute corners
rounded out, however, into the circular lines of Quentin's
"ripple" theory, which he formulates inwardly during his narrative session with Shreve at Harvard. Like any pebble
dropped into a pond, Quentin thinks, any human act sends
out ripples across the pond of the individual's life and beyond,
even to the lives of his counterparts in other generations and
ages, in an "ineradicable rhythm."

The pebble whose sinking begins the concentric ever-
widening ripples across the surface of Yoknapatawpha's time
and space, sending Quentin as actor and narrator in ever
shallower waves through the novels and short stories of the
Yoknapatawpha continuum—this stone could well be Quentin's own body falling into the Charles River. His suicide is of
central importance to both *The Sound and the Fury* and *Absalom, Absalom!* Beyond these Quentin is not a suicide, but he
provides the narrative voice and point of view for several fictions and reminiscences, the Quentin ripples spreading to the
earliest and latest of Faulkner's works but having, as they

move outward from the two novels, ever less reference to the biographic details of Quentin's identity as brother of Caddy and Harvard roommate of Shreve McKenzie (or McCannon).

It is almost fortunate for this discussion that most of Faulkner's short stories have not been reliably dated. If their dates of composition were known it would be easy to forget that Faulkner, like Quentin, had "always known" these stories; and it would be tempting to "organize" them into a chronology, a straight line, which would destroy the ripple figure Quentin himself provided.

Quentin's suicide, which sets him apart from the other Quentin and explains the divided youth who sits before Rosa Coldfield listening to "old ghost tales" at the beginning of *Absalom, Absalom!*, seems actually a little out of character with Don's friend and the other Quentin avatars whose greatest consistency is in their love of good tales and telling.

Even in *The Sound and the Fury* Quentin's suicide, completely convincing as it is to the reader, is out of character—at least as Quentin's character is remembered by Benjy and others. Benjy's big brother was fond of dogs and horses; the dogs obeyed him. Benjy's Quentin took action when action was required, hustling Benjy off to the barn and rebuking Luster when Benjy's howling disrupted Caddy's wedding reception. Obviously, from his long conversation with Quentin about Caddy's lost virtue, Mr. Compson did not think his son, distraught though he was then, would take his own life. Nor did Caddy.

But it is Quentin the suicide Faulkner's readers remember. That Quentin, defined by his death, appears only in the two novels to which his death is as central as it is to all the fictions of Yoknapatawpha and all the fictions of the American South.

Quentin Compson

Heir to a vanished fortune and a proud name already degenerated to idiocy and dishonor, broken-hearted and inadequately supported, forced to contemplate the dead unknowable past which could but will not explain his tragedy by explaining Henry Sutpen's, this Quentin embodies all the Southern fictionalists of his generation—and maybe all Southerners.

Although Quentin's suicide initiates the ripple spread which extends to the limits of Yoknapatawpha and beyond, it is the other Quentin, the born-and-bred story-teller, who is manifested in most of the ripples, including those of *Absalom, Absalom!* Then, after a series of shallower narrative performances, the ripples rise again to wave size with a resurgence of biographical references, and the Quentin figure becomes once more both narrator and protagonist. Caddy's unhappy brother plunges into the Charles River and out of Time, but eventually William Faulkner, who never had a sister, walks out onto the shore of Yoknapatawpha County remembering simultaneously his own and Quentin's childhoods and creating from their combination the boy Lucius Priest in *The Reivers,* subtitled *A Reminiscence.*

III

Continuums within Continuums:
The Legends of Sutpen, Part I

The name Sutpen is important to the unpublished story "Evangeline," to one well-known story, "Wash," to the novel *Absalom, Absalom!*, and to a preliminary filmscript, "Revolt in the Earth." In other Yoknapatawpha fiction the name is occasionally mentioned along with Compson, Sartoris, and deSpain as one of the oldest families in the county; and in Faulkner's last novel, *The Reivers*, there is fleeting reference to the founding of Sutpen's Hundred.[1]

"Evangeline" and "Wash" are integral parts of *Absalom, Absalom!*, but only "Wash" was published outside the novel. It is clear that Faulkner, who used most of his characters in many different fictions, benefitted comparatively little from the Sutpens as fictional resources, although they are an interesting family. Perhaps their shortcomings as literary subjects can be discovered by reviewing Faulkner's uses of them, both published and unpublished. This in turn should show, if only by implication, what it is about their use in *Absalom, Absalom!* that makes their legend viable there when it failed elsewhere.

---

[1] For "Evangeline," see Note 5, Chapter II; "Wash," *Harper's*, CLXVIII (February 1934) and in *Collected Stories*; "Revolt in the Earth," carbon typescript, Manuscript Collection, University of Virginia; *The Reivers* (Random House, 1962).

"Evangeline" is essentially the story improvised by Quentin and Shreve in the second half of *Absalom, Absalom!* but without the incest motif. It is the story of Judith and Henry Sutpen and Charles Bon, and its recent discovery reveals that the legends of Sutpen began not with the founder of Sutpen's Hundred and his "design" of establishing a dynasty, as critics have generally assumed, but with Judith, her brother Henry, and her brother's friend Charles Bon. As in *Absalom, Absalom!* it is a haunted house story in which a pair of young men patch the story together from fragments of information and one of them confronts the "ghost." The young men here are Don and "I."

The story begins with a ten-word telegram sent by Don to his friend. The narrator says in the first sentence of the story that he had not seen Don for seven years; the irrelevance of this statement—its "tacked-on" quality—and the fact that the telegram comes from a town unknown even to the narrator, a native of Mississippi, suggests that "Evangeline" was indeed written or drafted even before *Sartoris* and the earliest of the Yoknapatawpha tales.

Don in this story is an architect and an artist. He has come upon the old Sutpen place and learned that it is "haunted," so he wires his friend to join him at the obscure town's only hotel and to investigate the ghost.

The narrator joins Don in the little rural hotel. It is summer and very hot. The dollar-a-day room is sparsely furnished, and from the ceiling hangs a lone, bare light bulb. The friends have some inferior whiskey and they get a bucket of ice with which to tone it down. Don has stripped off his shirt in the heat to tell his friend about the haunted house. (This is the unexpected origin of Shreve's shirtlessness in the cold New England dormitory where he and Quentin collaborate on the same story developed in "Evangeline" by Don and his friend.)

Don's source of information has been an old Negro woman—not the oldest one on the Sutpen place, but the oldest woman's daughter. The story is so compounded of Southern literary clichés that his listener finishes Don's sentences for him, mocking Don's eager romanticism. The two establish a friendly competition in supplying details of the story, scoring points against each other for "correct" contributions, losing points for wrong ones. The young journalist ("I") gradually becomes involved, though, and as a narrative tension builds Don observes that his collaborator has ceased to try for points.

When he came upon the house, Don says, he found only Negroes living there, and only Negro women—no males at all over eleven years of age. The oldest of the women, "a regular empress," lives apart in a little cabin from which she oversees the activities of all the others. Don says the old Negress is named Sutpen.

The old woman's daughter, herself ancient, has told Don that her mother once talked "on and on" about the days of the plantation's grandeur and about the tragedy of Judith Sutpen, whose husband rode off to war on the very day of their wedding and was brought back to Judith by her brother at the end of the conflict "killed by the last shot of the war." This is one of the clichés the narrator has on the tip of his tongue.

But the woman's mother stopped talking about these things twenty-five years before Don found the place and the story. Now she claims that certain things she once talked about freely did not happen at all; her daughter cannot tell whether she remembers things from her childhood or has only heard her mother talk about them (and later deny them).

The Legends of Sutpen, Part I

Young Judith Sutpen's suitors, the woman said, came from "30 and 40 and 50" miles around "and one came further than that: Charles Bon. He and Judith's brother were the same age. They had met one another at school . . . ." Here the narrator loses a point by guessing the boys attended the University of Virginia.

At the University of Mississippi, less than a day's ride from home, Henry Sutpen kept a pair of saddle horses, a groom, and a German shepherd dog; and after boasting about his pretty sister to his friend Charles Bon, Henry brought Bon home for a weekend.

When Don reaches the part of his tale where the two young men ride up to the porch together, "and Judith leans against the column in a white dress—," his collaborator adds "With a red rose in her black hair—." "All right," says Don, "Have a rose," and Faulkner adds in the margin of the draft, "But she is blonde."

In this story Charles Bon is an orphan with a guardian in New Orleans. It is quickly decided that he and Judith will be married, but not until after Bon's graduation from college. At the end of the school year Bon goes away carrying Judith's portrait in a case "that closes like a book and locks with a key, and [he] left behind him a ring."

The following summer Henry visits Charles Bon in New Orleans. He plans to be away from home a month (in other lines of the same story, three months), but he returns in three weeks and makes Judith take off Bon's ring—but he refuses to say why.

Don continues the story as he learned it from the Negro woman: Judith refuses to obey her brother. Both she and their father (who has a very minor part in "Evangeline") demand an explanation, but Henry steadfastly refuses. "If they

33

[Judith and Henry]'d a had pistols they would a been just like Marse Henry and Charles on that Christmas morning the next year," the woman has told Don, for in this early version of the legend Henry and Charles did confront each other in a duel.

Back at school after the catastrophic visit to New Orleans, Charles and Henry no longer room together. They are not even on speaking terms; but the Sutpens, unable to make Henry explain, invite Charles Bon to their home for Christmas. At a holiday ball Judith's father announces her engagement, an engagement the guests knew about anyway, and Henry storms out of the room. He and his father argue loudly in the library, the colonel demanding Henry's reason for objecting to the engagement, Henry refusing to tell.

That night the colonel (his antebellum title is not explained) is wakened and rushes downstairs to find Henry and Charles squaring off with pistols. Close on her father's heels is Judith in her nightdress. In the preliminary draft the duel is in or near the house. In the "finished" story Bon and Henry face each other in the pasture; Colonel Sutpen, with his nightshirt stuffed into his pants and his suspenders flapping, rides a mule to the scene and Judith follows on a pony.

Both father and sister berate Henry for his incomprehensible behavior, and Charles Bon taunts Henry over his weakness in handling the dilemma of objection and loyalty.

For his insubordination Henry is told he had better leave home. He rides off without taking leave of his mother (the first mention of Mrs. Sutpen, and this only in the later, typed, version of the story) and without waiting for breakfast. He is not seen again for three years.

The wedding of Judith Sutpen and Charles Bon is scheduled for a year after Charles's graduation, but when the date

34

approaches, the Civil War has begun. Henry returns home, preparing to join the Army of the Confederacy. He and Judith are not speaking. He has been at home only three days when word comes that Charles Bon is at the hotel in town. Henry rides to town, where he and Charles reach an agreement. As a result of their bargaining Henry permits the wedding, but he and Charles ride off to war together late on the day of the ceremony. The marriage is not consummated, and either one or both of the young men seem hopeful that Bon will die in the conflict, allowing Henry to keep forever to himself the unspeakable secret he learned in New Orleans.

As the war begins badly for the South, Henry's father rounds up "the first four hundred men he met," pronounces them a regiment and himself its leader, and rides off to war leaving his wife, his daughter, and the Negro women to fend for themselves—"not leaning on the columns and not crying either."

His informant has also described for Don the confrontation of brother and sister when Henry brought Charles's body back at the close of the war: Judith is in white although her mother has died and she might be expected to have found a black dress somewhere even in hard times. A Negro runs into the house calling Missy, Missy, and Henry confronts his sister just inside the front door. This is Don's replay of the scene: " 'I've brought Charles home,' Henry says. She looks at him, the light is on her face, but not on his. Maybe it is his eyes talk, because he says, not moving, not even gesturing with his head: 'Out yonder. In the wagon.' "

The woman has told Don that when she was a child, after the deaths of Bon, Mrs. Sutpen, the colonel, and finally Judith—and long after the disappearance of Henry—her mother left her by accident in the big house, where she became frightened and tripped in the dark hall. Lying on her back on the floor she had looked up at a face "upside-down" hovering over her. She has led Don to believe that the face and the mansion's ghost are one and the same, but Don and his friend cannot tell who the presence in the house might be. Is it Judith? or Henry? or someone else? They even consider that it might be Henry's dog.

A fifty-year-old German shepherd? chides the newspaper man, "and *its* name is Sutpen, too." They think Henry's dog must have been dead when Henry went to war, but by some means successive generations of German shepherds have kept strangers, including tax collectors, away. Don tells of a neighbor's finding "the dog" dead in a ditch only to be attacked by a German shepherd when he approached what he supposed would be an unguarded house.

Faulkner's use of the German shepherd dogs is skillful and very effective, especially in the longer version of the story, where they are more important to the plot than in the earlier, shorter, version. The dog Henry kept at the university is supposed to have been the first of its breed in Mississippi, "descended from a pair brought back" from Germany by Henry's father (although in that case the colonel's dogs, not Henry's dog, would have been Mississippi's first). The reference to Colonel Sutpen's travel to Europe involving a return trip from Germany to Mississippi is not accommodated in the subsequent account of his life as it is given in *Absalom, Absalom!*

When Henry is banished from home, his dog gets into the house and will let no one approach Henry's room for several days.

The dog guarding the Sutpen house some sixty years later

when Don and his friend appear on the scene is no ghost, says
Don. He has seen it, "and it's a flesh and blood dog." At the
end of the story, when the house is destroyed by fire, this
dog's howling supplies the accompaniment to catastrophe supplied in *Absalom, Absalom!* by the howling of Charles Bon's
idiot grandson, Jim Bond.

Because Don's friend has proclaimed his disbelief in ghosts
and because dogs like him (as they liked Quentin in *The
Sound and the Fury*), Don has called his friend in and now expects him to go to the haunted house, cope with the dog, and
answer his own question, "Who do you suppose is living in
that house?"

"And so I did what Don said. I went there and I went into
that house. And I was right and Don was right. That dog was
a flesh and blood dog and that ghost was a flesh and blood
ghost. It had lived in that house for fifty years" (fifty in the au-
tograph copy—forty in the finished story—only four in *Absalom, Absalom!*), "with the old negro woman supplying it with
food, and no man the wiser."

All the information Don gives his friend in Part I of
"Evangeline"—the story is in seven parts—has come from the
Negro woman whose mother bears the name of Sutpen.
When the narrator approaches the Sutpen place in the second
section of the story, he goes not to Don's informant (in one of
the fragments among the papers of the Jill Faulkner Summers
Archive this woman is named Sukey), but to her mother.
Looking at the old woman he concludes that she is not Negro
but Indian—and Sutpen. The other Negroes around the Sutpen house are characterized as darker and darker depending
on how far their generations are removed from the matriarch.

The young man tells the old woman, at her cabin, that he is

"a writer, a man that writes pieces for the newspaper, and such." She replies that he is not the first journalist to have tried to learn Sutpen secrets, but that the others could not get past the dog. He will have to pass the dog, she says, not expecting him to do it.

He gets rid of the dog by giving it a piece of raw meat wrapped around a handful of pepper which sends it streaking for the creek. He goes alone to the house and enters the dark first floor hall thinking that Judith will hear his entry and speak the name of the old woman—which he does not know. Instead the old woman herself comes up behind him and guides him upstairs in the dark and into a bedroom where a cadaverous old man lies with closed eyelids. The episode is even more compelling in "Evangeline" than in *Absalom, Absalom!* because the invalid does not—perhaps cannot—speak or indicate in any way that he is aware of his visitor.

> "My God," I said. "Who is it?"
> "It's Henry Sutpen," she said.

Downstairs, in the dark kitchen, the old woman, whose name is Raby, tells her somewhat shaken inquisitor that Henry has been near death for nearly a week. Through the years of his hiding Henry had walked abroad at night with the dog, and a week before the arrival of Don and his friend the dog's howling had brought her to Henry where he had fallen. (As his dogs died one after the other, Henry would make a two-day journey on foot to replace them. Raby says he was young "then" but for the last dog she had made the trip herself.)

Raby had got Henry to bed, although her guest cannot understand where she found the strength, and she expects

Henry to die soon, maybe before morning. The narrator asks why she has not sent for the doctor, but she is not willing to consider it. He offers to stay and help her with the inevitable burial, but she says she will bury Henry as she has buried "the others" without assistance.

During their talk Henry's dog approaches the house twice. The first time Raby speaks to it and stills it. The second time the narrator steps to the window, speaks to the dog, and quiets it.

Having admitted the young man to her secrets, Raby "talked, not more rapidly exactly. I dont know how to express it. It was like a train running along a track, not fast, but you got off the track." She tells him, more or less as her daughter told Don, about Judith and Henry and Charles Bon, especially about Henry's trip to New Orleans and his early return "because he had found it out."

What Henry found out was that Charles Bon was involved with another woman than Judith. Henry seems to have thought the woman was only a mistress, which would have been bad enough to Henry, but Charles Bon lied to Henry, says Raby. Bon was actually married to the woman.

"I wonder how Henry found out that Charles and the New Orleans woman were really married," the narrator ponders, but Raby will not tell.

She also withholds another piece of information, the reason Charles Bon needed a divorce from the New Orleans woman. It appears that Faulkner himself was having difficulties with both the facts and the chronology of his story. At this point, on second and later readings, it appears that Charles was unaware until the birth of his son that the child's mother was part Negro—in the manner of much nineteenth-century fiction. But the portrait which Bon substituted for Judith's in the picture case (mentioned but not "substantiated" in *Absalom, Absalom!*) revealed her racial make-up clearly enough to Judith and later to the narrator of "Evangeline." Various drafts and trial paragraphs of portions of *Absalom, Absalom!*— especially what seem efforts to get the novel started—were among the papers found with the "Evangeline" draft and typescript. They, like the draft of the short story, are cluttered with abandoned "facts," with changed dates, and with marginal calculations of the ages of various characters at various dates.

This section of the story is its least effective because of the scrambled plotting, all revealed (or omitted) in the dialogue between the narrator and Raby, but it establishes many of the elements retained in *Absalom, Absalom!* and provides, as do all the other sections of the story, even much of the novel's final wording. Significantly, it does *not* provide some of the novel's most important elements—most of them attributable only to the imaginations of Quentin and Shreve.

Raby reviews the war episodes of Judith's story—it is Judith she is most concerned for—including the arrival of Henry with Bon's body. She tells of hearing pounding noises from the room where Judith sat all night with her husband's body and of finding the picture case, battered shut, on the bed when she entered the room to help Judith prepare the body for burial. No, Judith tells her, the case is not to be buried with Charles.

Raby tells of the hard work she and Judith undertook to feed themselves and keep the plantation operating, of the death of Mrs. Sutpen during the war and of the colonel's death five years after the close of the war. She tells, also, of

Judith's correspondence with the New Orleans woman and of Judith's sending money for the woman to bring her child to visit Charles Bon's grave. (The child is six years old in the draft, nine in the finished story.) Then Judith continued to send money regularly to New Orleans in spite of her own hardships.

The appearance of the woman—her physical appearance—seems not to have been unusual (as the substituted portrait would indicate) but, says Raby, "as soon as I saw [the child] I knew. And as soon as Judith saw him she knew too." "Knew what?" the narrator wants to know, but Raby does not answer.

(Faulkner must have intended the child's Negro blood to have come from his mother, at least at this point in the development of the story; Charles Bon's lack of parents, however, makes the matter ambiguous. Bon's appearance is left to the imagination of the reader, but it seems never to have troubled any of the Sutpens.)

In Faulkner's expanded typescript of "Evangeline" Raby's scorn of the New Orleans woman is elaborated, as is Judith's stoicism. The visitor seems not to have realized that her hostess had married Charles Bon, and she is insensitive to the sacrifices Judith has made to honor his memory. Waited on by Judith and the Sutpen Negroes, she suggests improvements to be made in the property and in Judith's manner of living—improvements that are out of the question economically. Raby's hatred of her practically freezes the paper on which it is recorded.

After the departure of Bon's New Orleans wife and child, Judith voices her first complaint: "I'm so tired, Raby." Having realized the reason for Henry's objection to her marriage (not put into words by Raby or the narrator—just the fact of the child's mixed blood), Judith writes to Henry. She prepares a second letter and gives it to Raby, telling her that she will know when to mail it. Raby is illiterate, but she recognizes Henry's name on the envelope. Judith, worn out by her long ordeal, tells Raby to mail the letter at last, but Raby has already mailed it, for Judith is dying. Henry returns just before her death. "Henry, I'm so tired," says Judith.

Where Henry had been, what life he abandoned to come home, his motivation for hiding there for so many years— these are not revealed or implied. The narrator interrupts Raby's story to ask why she has so unselfishly cared for Henry all these years. He receives the same answer Quentin receives from Clytie in *Absalom, Absalom!*: "Henry Sutpen is my brother."

The old woman tells her visitor to leave. "You done found out now. You go on and write your paper piece." But he tells her that maybe he won't write it at all. He goes down the dark drive but comes back quietly, with some concern that the dog will announce his presence and the old woman will know he has lied to her about leaving as Bon lied to Henry about his marriage to the octoroon.

He sits on the top step of the veranda in the dark. He is still uneasy about the dog, but it appears without a sound, watches him a little while, and silently disappears.

In the deep shadows of the porch the narrator drifts into either sleep or revery, where he confronts young Charles Bon, and young Henry Sutpen, and old Raby. He questions them about Bon's death. The exchange is brief and inconclusive. He asks Bon, then Henry, who fired that last shot of the war. Henry concedes that he did fire "a last shot in the war."

The narrator is startled by the dog's howling. He stumbles

42

away from the steps to find the house in flames and the Negroes running toward it wailing and crying. The dog throws itself again and again at the front door barking and howling. Then all—dog, Negroes, and narrator—rush around to the back of the house only to find the fire more intense there than at the front. Back they surge to the front just in time to see Raby's face at an upstairs window. The structure collapses, and the dog—this is the one absolutely false note in the whole thing—without a sound hurls itself into the flaming wreckage.

The fire is quenched by a sudden downpour of rain which cools the embers sufficiently for the observers next day to attempt some sort of salvage. Raby's daughter, Don's informant, finds the picture case and claims it as "Sutpen property." The narrator talks her into letting him pry it open, promising to return it to her.

The case opens not at the battered lock but at the hinges, revealing instead of blond Judith "the smooth, oval, unblemished face, the mouth rich, full, a little loose, the hot slumbrous, secretive eyes, the inklike hair with its faint but unmistakable wiriness—all the ineradicable and tragic stamp of negro blood"—Charles Bon's octoroon—and the inscription A mon mari, Toujours, 12 Aout, 1860. (Faulkner changed the year as he typed, striking out 1857.)

The distasteful (in the late twentieth century) racial attitude embodied in these lines, and in the story itself, is held firmly in the nineteenth century where it belongs. The narrator looks sadly at the picture thinking that "to a Henry Sutpen born," given Henry's genteel-but-provincial Southern upbringing, the woman's Negro blood would have been "worse than the marriage" and would have "compounded the bigamy to where the pistol was not only justified, but inescapable."

Most of "Evangeline," plot and wording, went almost un-

modified into *Absalom, Absalom!* The story told by Raby and
her daughter was broken up and parcelled out among other
narrators—Quentin's father, Rosa Coldfield, and the secondary sources quoted by these two—and other short stories
were added, most of them about Thomas Sutpen's early days
in Mississippi and elsewhere. But "Evangeline" stops short.

Most important, since we are concerned with Quentin,
whose falsely self-proclaimed incest is so important in *The
Sound and the Fury*, "Evangeline" contains no suggestion that
a marriage between Judith Sutpen and Charles Bon would
have been either miscegenous or incestuous. In "Evangeline"
Henry's objection is that Bon's marriage to Judith would have
been morally bigamous, though the prior marriage, involving
miscegenation, was not legally binding in either Louisiana or
Mississippi. As for Bon's child and whatever its appearance
made clear, Henry never saw it—it had not been born when
he faced Bon in the duel.

In *Absalom, Absalom!* Mr. Compson, a lawyer, appreciates
the legally insupportable nature of Bon's alliance with an octoroon. He tells Quentin the "marriage" was insufficient reason for the murder. In "Evangeline" Henry Sutpen grudg-
ingly permits his sister's bigamous wedding ceremony hoping
that the marriage will never be consummated—whether he
had met the woman in New Orleans and knew or suspected
her Negro blood is not made clear. If he knew of it when he
opposed Charles Bon (he would have learned it from Judith
when they were reconciled before her death if he did not
know it before that), then Henry condoned Bon's bigamy but
balked at Bon's miscegenation. In *Absalom, Absalom!*, according to Quentin, *Judith* was threatened with miscegenation—and incest.

What interracial pairing "Evangeline" contains is between Sutpen and the unnamed mother of Raby, where it provides an ironic comment on Sutpen morality, and between Charles Bon and the mother of his child.

There are many faults in the plotting of "Evangeline," and most of them survived Quentin's tormented attempts to resolve them, but the story is often compelling, and it is a necessary step in the development of the novel. One passage is especially important. As the narrator muses on the steps of the crumbling veranda where Judith in a white dress with a red rose in her hair once leaned against perhaps the same column, he resigns himself to his inability to fathom the behavior of the legendary people who lived in the house before he was born, and the old man who is about to die in it.

"[M]aybe nowadays we can no longer understand people of that time," he thinks. "Perhaps that's why to us their written and told doings have a quality fustian though courageous; gallant, yet a little absurd." He lacks not only understanding, however. There is a piece of information missing: ". . . and I thought quietly, 'And now I'll never know that. And without it, the whole tale will be pointless, and so I am wasting my time.' "

This sounds more than a little like Mr. Compson's bewilderment in the shadows of his own veranda in *Absalom, Absalom!* when he is at a loss to explain Henry's murdering Bon:

> It's just incredible. It just does not explain . . . . Or perhaps that's it: they don't explain and we are not supposed to know. We have a few old mouth-to-mouth tales; we exhume from old trunks and boxes and drawers letters without salutation or signature, in which men and women who once lived and breathed are now merely initials or nicknames out of some now incomprehensible

affection which sound to us like Sanskrit or Chocktaw; we see dimly people, the people in whose living blood and seed we ourselves lay dormant and waiting, performing their acts of simple passion and simple violence, impervious to time and inexplicable—Yes, Judith, Bon, Henry, Sutpen: all of them. (*AA*, 100–101)

Aside from the judgment that "Evangeline" is a mass of nineteenth-century Southern-fiction clichés, perhaps its major weakness is suggested by the contrast between these two otherwise similar passages: in the story the "something more" which will "explain" everything *is found* and it is the Southern cliché to end all Southern clichés—mixed blood. In the novel, although the answer is "found," the route toward it is more important than the answer. Furthermore, the answer is presented as the product of Quentin's fancy—which is to say, as Sportin' Life sang, "It ain't necessarily so," and it does not terminate the mystery. Quentin's conclusions that Charles Bon was the half-brother of Henry and Judith Sutpen, that Charles's mother was part Negro, that Henry Sutpen killed his own brother to save his sister from an incestuous and miscegenous marriage—these say a great deal about Quentin's torment, brought forward from *The Sound and the Fury,* but they are not even intended to say anything about the characters brought to *Absalom, Absalom!* from "Evangeline."

Here a word about literary titles: it is deceptively easy to identify their sources and tempting to use them as springboards to explication of seemingly obvious analogies. There is only one Evangeline in literature that I know of, but Longfellow's poem about the long search of Evangeline Bellefontaine for her fiance, Gabriel Lajeunesse (aside from the separation of the lovers) has little in common with Faulkner's short story. The title is the same, of course, and Faulkner evidently used it as a pointer of some sort or a means of setting the tone of his own "Evangeline."

I have found only one coincidental connection between the poem and the novel *Absalom, Absalom!*—a name—indicating Faulkner's familiarity with the poem. He would have read it, as almost everyone else in America read it until well into the twentieth century, as a school assignment. When Evangeline Bellefontaine was about seventeen, in the idyllic Nova Scotian village of Grand Pré,

> "Sunshine of Saint Eulalie" was she called;
> for that was the sunshine
> Which, as the farmers believed, would
> load their orchards with apples;
> She, too, would bring to her husband's house
> delight and abundance,
> Filling it full of love and the ruddy
> faces of children.

When Faulkner prepared the chronology and genealogy which he appended to *Absalom, Absalom!* he found Charles Bon's mother needed a name. He entered her in the genealogy as Eulalia.

A likely link between the poem and the story was available to Faulkner closer to Mississippi and to New Orleans, where Faulkner shared William Spratling's living quarters for a while. The Evangeline legend in Louisiana concerns an Acadian girl, Longfellow's model, Emmeline Labiche. This young woman followed her fiance from Canada down the Mississippi River into Cajun country. There she found him married to another woman, and Emmeline went mad. Her grave and a statue are located in Longfellow-Evangeline Memorial Park at St. Martinville. On the base of the statue is the name Evangeline.

Equally will-o-the-wisp is the title *Absalom, Absalom!*, especially since the biblical story of Absalom includes an incestuous and fratricidal triangle of two half-brothers and their sister. Several ingenious studies have equated Thomas Sutpen, of all people, to King David, whose fifty sons and fifty daughters certainly left his dynasty beyond the need of further begetting.[2]

The assignment of biblical roles to Judith and Henry and Charles Bon is more problematical than the assignment of Sutpen to the role of King David. David's cry of grief is for Absalom, not Amnon, and it was Amnon, not Absalom, who coldly calculated and accomplished the rape of his sister. Shall Henry Sutpen be Amnon or Absalom? Shall Charles Bon be Absalom or Amnon? Judith, of course, gets the female lead, Tamar, victim not of a questionable betrothal but of a brutal rape.

It is as easy to find the flaws in such an analogical effort as it is tempting to make the effort in the first place.

"Absalom, Absalom!" is simply a parent's cry of grief for a lost son, a favorite. As such it has been used so often it has become synonymous with another fragment of wording in the same ancient lament, "My son, my son!" An example of the exclamation's general acceptance as a simple expression of parental grief is found in *An American Tragedy*. There Theo-

[2] 2 Sam. 13–19. Absalom's is a two-part story: first is the incest and fratricide story of Amnon, Tamar, and Absalom; after that comes the rebellion against King David led by Absalom, Absalom's death against his father's orders, and the lamentation of David for his favorite—whom he neither renounced nor refused to acknowledge.

dore Dreiser used the name Absalom in reference to probably the least heroic character in all of American literature.

At the time of Clyde Griffiths' trial for murder, his mother, a poorly educated but devout evangelist, does her best to support him. "But 'Jehoval, jirah,' " she pleads, " 'Thou wilt not require of a mother [that she doubt her son] Oh, no—Thou wilt not. O Lamb of God, Thou wilt not!' She turned: she bruised under her heel the scaly head of this dark suspicion—as terrifying to her as his guilt was to him. 'O Absalom, my Absalom!' " [3]

David's long and unrestrained lamentation for Absalom is given in the Old Testament. "O my son Absalom," wailed the king, "my son, Absalom! Would God I had died for thee, O Absalom, my son, my son!" The intensity of David's grief for Absalom has been recognized for centuries and his words have been used for centuries by anguished parents. But Thomas Sutpen, as Faulkner characterized him throughout the novel and in Sutpen's other brief Yoknapatawpha appearances, never felt such intense love or loss for anyone. We cannot even decide whether his Absalom would have been Charles Bon, whom he is supposed to have abandoned when Charles was an infant or refused to acknowledge even privately when Charles was grown, or Henry Sutpen, his legitimate heir who was sent away from home for objecting to his sister's engagement.

In contrast, for readers who associate *Absalom, Absalom!* with *The Sound and the Fury,* Jason Compson felt keenly the distress of his son Quentin, and within a few months of Quentin's suicide, Jason himself had died.

[3] Theodore Dreiser, *An American Tragedy* (New York: Signet, 1964), 749. Originally published by Horace Liveright, Inc., 1925.

IV

Continuums within Continuums:
The Legends of Sutpen, Part II

At least as important to *Absalom, Absalom!* as any of the other elements derived from "Evangeline" is one which appears in two of the other Don-and-I stories and in both the novels to which Quentin is important. A suggestion of it might be seen in a story at least as old as the Don-and-I tales, "Selvage," expanded and published in 1934 as "Elly." [1] It is the theme of the murdered bridegroom.

Faulkner's treatments of this theme vary so, and it is always so subordinated to other strongly emotional elements of the fiction that the theme has received little or no notice, although it is, by my count, used more often in works contributing to *Absalom, Absalom!* (including *The Sound and the Fury*) than miscegenation, incest, or the rise and fall of a Southern aristocracy—all of which have been put forward as primary themes of *Absalom, Absalom!* The widow-but-not-bride is mentioned often enough by Faulkner in his own voice as well as by his surrogate narrators, but nobody seems to notice the murdered—not slain, as in battle, murdered—man whose young widow is as much a stock character in Southern

---

[1] "Selvage," Manuscript Collection, University of Virginia; "Elly," *Story*, IV (February 1934), also in *Doctor Martino and Other Stories* (New York: Smith and Hass, 1934), and in *Collected Stories*.

romantic fiction as Colombine is in classic pantomime. (Fratricide, a seeming "natural" for a novel of America's fratricidal war, has no part in any of these works except *Absalom, Absalom!* itself, where it is introduced by Quentin.)

In "Selvage" and "Elly" the young man who loses his life is not a bridegroom—he has firmly resisted that position—but he has seduced the girl who kills him and been seduced by her. The man, a New Orleans Creole, is vaguely suggestive of Charles Bon, but only because he is from New Orleans. Elly's intention, or impulse, is to kill herself with the man who refuses to marry her and to kill also her hidebound old grandmother, whom she hates and blames for her unhappiness. She grabs the steering wheel of the car in which they are all riding, but only the man and the grandmother die in the wrecked car.

The murdered bridegroom appears more insistently in three of the four Don-and-I stories. There and in the two novels Faulkner's fictive hovering over the motif of the murdered groom, always burying it in the story's past and giving "present" matters closer attention, suggests that the motif was buzzing around in his mind like a tune for which he could not remember the title or words and which he could not get rid of either.

In "Evangeline" the dead bridegroom is, of course, Charles Bon. "Mistral" and "Snow" are the other Don-and-I stories about murdered grooms. In setting, plot, and structure they are companion pieces, almost too much alike for there to have been two different stories.

In "Mistral" the two pedestrian travelers approach an Italian village just ahead of the local weather phenomenon, the cruel wind called *mistral*, and find a funeral in progress. On the same day a young soldier, having completed his military service, returns to his lover in the village. The girl is the ward of the local priest. She is also the "widow but not bride" of the man being buried. Her intended husband is said to have died suddenly of an undiagnosed illness.

An elderly native of the region tells Don and the narrator that the girl's foster father is attracted to her by emotions inappropriate for a spiritual or a foster father, let alone a natural father. (One easy interpretation of the story would have the priest the girl's natural father.) The dead bridegroom, Don and his friend feel sure, was poisoned either by the girl herself or by someone else on behalf of the young lovers.

In addition to the murdered groom, this story contains the strong suggestion of incest. The young collaborators, Don and his friend, ponder what it must have been like for the priest watching the girl mature under his own protection, and Don says he hopes he will never have a daughter. The narrator's comments on their youth and its intensification of their emotional involvement with the tragedy of passion unfolding before them, a drama in which they have no legitimate business, as well as Don's remarks about "what it must be like," are suggestive of Shreve's and Quentin's easy identification with Henry Sutpen and Charles Bon—also, ironically, of Jason Compson's (Quentin's brother's) agitation over his niece in *The Sound and the Fury*.

As in many of Faulkner's other published stories that can be compared with their own earlier unpublished versions, "Mistral" was lengthened and complicated in revision by the addition of several secondary narrators and by the multiplication of incidents.

In "Snow" the travelers have moved on northward and

approach a Swiss village. Again there is about to be a funeral. Using a one-eyed "pair" of binoculars they have bought in a pawn shop, the young friends observe a party of mountain climbers bringing the body of a man down from a high peak. Walking on into the town, they go, as in "Mistral," first to the church and then to a restaurant or inn, gathering information from people with whom they come in contact. Also as in "Mistral," they learn that the man's death has very nearly coincided with his wedding, but in this case it came just after rather than just before the ceremony. The body has been in the high snow all winter, the accident having happened on the last day of climbing weather the preceding autumn. Among the mourners is a stylishly dressed young woman whom the Americans take to be Parisian; but they are told she is a native of the village, the widow of the dead man, in fact.

A waiter who has lived in America tells them that the man who died on the mountain was a professional climber named Brix. On the morning of Brix's wedding one of his clients, a German who had been coming to the Swiss village to climb the easier peaks for several years, came unexpectedly to town and wanted to hire Brix, as usual, as his guide. Somehow the man's wish prevailed, and Brix, his bride, his partner Emil Hiller, and the German made up a party. The German offered to provide a wedding supper at their first stop on the mountain. The waiter continues:

> "So they climbed to the Bernardines' and the Big Shot gave the wedding supper and the next morning they are on the *glacis* where Brix hadn't intended to be except that something had gone wrong, the weather probably, . . . Anyway the Big Shot is where Brix shouldn't have taken him, doing whatever it was that Brix and Hiller should have known he would do, and he goes off the

ledge and takes Mrs. Brix with him and the two of them take Brix
and so there they are: Hiller anchored on the ledge with his end
of the rope, and Mrs. Brix and then the Big Shot and then Brix at
the other end of it dangling down the ice-face."

Knowing that his partner cannot pull three adults to safety,
Brix cuts the rope between himself and the German. After
the safe descent of the survivors, rescue efforts are made, the
German client having offered "a good piece of jack for finding
Brix," but in vain.

Strangest of all, the widow-bride left town with the German
the morning after the accident. Neither Don and the narrator
nor their informant can explain that.

With spring thaws Hiller has sent word to the German, the
young woman has returned to the village, and she and Hiller
have found the body. She stays all night in the church with
her husband's body and leaves town again shortly after the
funeral.

In a peculiar one-page fragment among the Rowan Oak
papers,[2] a man talks with a judge "from Mississippi in
America." He asks if the judge has seen "her"—she promised
to come. He refers to "the patron," who seems to have been
wearing leather britches. As he "passed" the patron and "her"
"on the way down," she called out "Emil, Emil!"

In the fragment, Emil might be the name of the speaker—
it seems to be—but in "Snow" Emil Hiller is the surviving
partner. The man tells the judge that he "confessed to her"
past the leather (or leather-colored) seat of the patron and
called back to her as he passed that "It doesn't matter," because the priest had said that morning that life is important,
not "what comes after."

[2] The Jill Faulkner Summers Archive.

Perhaps Faulkner at one point intended to carry his story on to a legal investigation of Brix's death (though why a judge from Mississippi in America?). If so, Emil's confession (of what?) to the woman occurred after his partner's fall and while the survivors climbed down the mountain, or in the spring when they brought the body down. In this case, the judge and Emil are talking in the village at the time of the funeral. Otherwise Emil is the man who fell—this is how the fragment "feels"—and he is meeting the judge in some sort of afterlife, but this does not seem like Faulkner.

At any rate, in "Snow," as in the other stories, Don and his friend have found a story but not all its details. Like their other stories, this one is framed by the narrator's reminiscence of an episode in his journey with Don.

But the frame of "Snow" has a frame of its own, and that outer frame offers a surprising connection between "Snow" and *The Sound and the Fury*. The narrator in the outer frame is Don's friend, but the time is fifteen years after the Swiss funeral, the beginning of World War II.

The narrator here is "an architect, successful, a husband and father, in his late thirties." The day after Pearl Harbor he "dug up the old records of the military school of his youth" and is now awaiting his first assignment as "a subaltern of engineers."

The man and his child are looking at two photographs in a newspaper and "what was not even a column head on that inside page but just a caption: *Nazi Governor of Czodnia Slain by Companion*." The man recognizes the Nazi's companion as the widow of the Swiss mountain climber. Her face is "a little older than when he had seen it fifteen years ago and no longer a peasant's face now." Evidently she has waited fifteen years for just the right moment to avenge her husband's death—if, indeed, the German was somehow to blame.

The narrator's child, meanwhile, has asked about the seemingly universal distrust of Germans. Was it different before the war? Remembering the Swiss villagers' antipathy toward Brix's German client and toward the young widow who went off with him, the father answers that it has always been the same.

(It should be mentioned that when this obviously updated story was submitted for publication in 1942, its blatant chauvinism toward the national enemy was not only acceptable but—or so it seemed then—in the national interest, a morale builder . . . or something. It seems, nevertheless, to have been the cause of the story's editorial rejection, for "Snow" is really a pretty good story, its anti-German touch as "tacked-on" as the outer frame.)

It is the newsphotos of a German military governor and his mistress, of course, that are familiar to Faulkner's readers. Faulkner used the outer frame of "Snow" in the appendix he prepared for Malcolm Cowley's *The Portable Faulkner* (Random House, 1945). There, in the Compson Appendix, a single newsphoto shows a German general and his mistress in an open touring car in the Alps. Jefferson's librarian recognizes the woman as Caddy Compson, the sister of Quentin (who has been dead for thirty years) and of Jason, the last Compson in the town. She takes the newspaper to Jason, who admits that it is Caddy, all right, before he realizes that denial is the more prudent reaction. He has not seen Caddy since his father's funeral shortly after Quentin's.

"The Big Shot," the Swiss waiter's name for the German client in "Snow," is the title of the remaining narrative by Don and his friend. Here the important man, the big shot, is

Dal Martin, a Memphis gangster. Martin has been Don's source and is his subject. The unnamed narrator provides the briefest possible introduction and a single question at the end. There is no murdered bridegroom in this one, but the pattern of Dal Martin's grand design, springing from his rebuff at the door of a rich man's house when he was a boy, his design of raising himself economically and socially to the level, or above it, of the owner of the mansion, this is quite clearly the pattern of Thomas Sutpen's design for his life. Thomas Sutpen, too, was turned away from the front door of a mansion. He tells Quentin's grandfather about it in *Absalom, Absalom!* during the hunt for his runaway French architect.

"The Big Shot" contributed incidents, themes, and characters to several successfully published works by Faulkner. It is, for instance, the first appearance of the notorious Popeye of *Sanctuary*.

After its rejection early in 1930, Faulkner revised "The Big Shot" and sent it out under the truly self-defeating title "A Dull Tale." ("A Dull Tale" contains a minor interesting echo from *The Sound and the Fury*: the echo of Caddy's wedding slippers on the stairs as she runs to comfort Benjy. Martin's daughter returns from a party to which he had connived an invitation for her; she is weeping, running, "her heels brittle and hard.")

The murdered bridegroom of *Absalom, Absalom!* itself is, as in "Evangeline," Charles Bon, although in the novel his wedding to Judith is omitted and it is a dead fiance Henry Sutpen brings home to his sister.

Even in *The Sound and the Fury* there are two enactments of the murdered bridegroom theme, neither effective, and in both Quentin is the would-be perpetrator. First, Quentin fails in a perfectly good opportunity to shoot Dalton Ames, Caddy's lover, with Ames's own pistol. Later, during preparations for Caddy's wedding to Sidney Herbert Head, Quentin *wishes* to be rid of the bridegroom. He fancies a voice saying *Quentin has shot Herbert he shot his voice through the floor of Caddy's room.*

When Faulkner was trying to use Don and his nameless friend, and then a pair of their talk-alikes named Chisholm and Burke, in a novel-length version of "Evangeline," he must have been wanting all along to use Quentin by name, for the two pairs of friends are, as I have tried to show, basically Shreve and Quentin figures. Quentin, having endured but not resolved his ordeal of August 1909, would have seen good reason to murder the bridegroom in almost *any* story, but "Evangeline" was made to order for him. But Quentin was dead.

The new novel came alive when Faulkner realized that he could fit it into Quentin's last year, a perfect fit and perfectly appropriate. And Quentin brought with him to the new fiction what the narrator of "Evangeline" could not find—a plausible explanation of the murder of Charles Bon by Henry Sutpen, the threat not of miscegenation but of incest.

Among the Sutpen stories Quentin tells his Harvard roommate in *Absalom, Absalom!* (as he has heard it from his father, who heard it from *his* father) is the story of how Wash Jones killed Thomas Sutpen with a scythe because of his disappointment in Sutpen's character. (In a way, Sutpen himself is a kind of murdered bridegroom—like Elly's Creole he is murdered for refusing to be a bridegroom.)

Because "Wash" is the only published short story to name Thomas Sutpen, it was long thought to be the cornerstone of

Absalom, Absalom!, but it is hard to tell whether "Wash" was written before or after "Evangeline" and "The Big Shot"—or even before the main part of the novel. As James B. Meriwether acknowledges in the introduction to his bibliography of Faulkner's stories, it is hard to distinguish the stories Faulkner incorporated into his novels from those he sold for publication independently of their parent novels.[3]

Writing about Faulkner's unfinished novel *Elmer* and the short story "Portrait of Elmer," Thomas L. McHaney makes the same point and adds in a footnote that "there is startling evidence in Faulkner's early work that most of his characters and thematic preoccupations existed in his mind almost from the beginning of his career."[4] McHaney illustrates this with Faulkner's statement that the Wash story in *Absalom, Absalom!* came from his Snopes material. McHaney's amazement must be founded on the later (than *Absalom, Absalom!*) dates of the Snopes trilogy, but as a matter of fact Faulkner is known to have put aside or postponed the first Snopes novel, presumably the one that became *The Hamlet*, in favor of *Absalom, Absalom!* This leads on to the supposition that "Wash" could just as easily have wound up in a Snopes novel as in a Compson novel (*the* Sutpen novel). It also points up the extreme difficulty of tracing any thematic or substantive thread through Faulkner's work, which is not—McHaney's comment is well-founded—a sequence but a galaxy of continuums.

As to whether "Wash" is a Snopes-style story or a founda-

[3] "The Short Fiction of William Faulkner: A Bibliography," *PROOF: The Yearbook of American Bibliographical and Textual Studies*, ed. Joseph Katz, Vol. I (Columbia, S.C.: University of South Carolina Press, 1971).

[4] "The Elmer Papers: Faulkner's Comic Portrait of the Artist," *Mississippi Quarterly: Special Issue, William Faulkner*, XXVI, 3 (Summer 1973), note 8, p. 284.

tion for *Absalom, Absalom!*, both the internal evidence of the story and its use in the novel favor the Snopes orientation. For *Absalom, Absalom!*, it seems, Faulkner took the relatively unimportant figure of Colonel Sutpen in "Evangeline" to tell in "Wash" how and why at the last possible moment, when Sutpen's crumbling design could have been restored by the birth of a son, Wash Jones killed Sutpen. By showing the old colonel's reaction to the birth of his last "get"—a girl— Faulkner developed facets of Sutpen's character which were important to *Absalom, Absalom!*—Sutpen's obsession with the need for a male heir, and his callousness in rejecting Wash Jones's granddaughter for having borne him a daughter instead of the son he wanted.

"Wash" is a good story well told, and it deserves the distinction of being the only one of the stories previewing *Absalom, Absalom!* to have been published outside the novel; but it does little to establish Thomas Sutpen as a figure more worthy than his children, Judith and Henry, to be the subject of the Sutpen myth or legends.

Sutpen's coldly casual rejection of the ignorant girl who bore his child on a pallet on the floor of her grandfather's cabin may have been deliberate provocation of the grandfather; and if so it was tantamount to suicide, but the story, as its title accurately indicates, is not Sutpen's tragedy—it is Wash Jones's.

Abruptly disillusioned by his erstwhile hero, Wash is transformed from servile water-bearer into Fate personified. Although he is nothing but "poor white trash," Wash is magnificent in comparison to the man he literally cuts down. Wash dramatizes his disappointment in a flood of violence—his murder of Sutpen, then his murders of the young mother and her child, and finally his scythe-swinging charge into the guns of the sheriff's men. By contrast, Sutpen's despair over his lost effort to reestablish a dynasty is barely intimated.

It is hard to see how critics could have been satisfied with "Wash" as a foundation for *Absalom, Absalom!* even before the discovery of "Evangeline." The basic function of "Wash" in the novel is to counteract, not to support, the notion that Thomas Sutpen was either heroic or demonic. It serves to disabuse the reader, as Wash Jones was disabused, of any belief that the man Sutpen was worthy of admiration or sympathy— or book-length commemoration.

After *Absalom, Absalom!* Faulkner made only one attempt to reuse the Sutpen material. For this attempt he dispensed with Quentin and all other narrators probably because narrators are not easily manageable in dramatic media, and this was a preliminary script for a film.

The title page of "Revolt in the Earth" bears the names of both William Faulkner and Dudley Murphy. The work was rejected diplomatically but firmly by Warner Brothers' Robert Buckner, who sent the typescript back to Faulkner with a note indicting it as "badly conceived" and having "no possibilities whatever for a motion picture." In his note Buckner refused to acknowledge that Faulkner had had a hand in the writing and hoped "if you had nothing to do with it that you will not let it get around with your name on it." [5]

Blotner, in his biography of Faulkner, reports this rejection, but he takes Buckner's transparent diplomacy at face value.

Both Blotner and Tom Dardis (*Some Time in the Sun,*

---

[5] A carbon typescript of "Revolt in the Earth," with Robert Buckner's note paperclipped to it, is in the Manuscript Collection of the University of Virginia.

Scribner's, 1976) have mentioned Faulkner's efforts to sell screen rights to *Absalom, Absalom!* while the novel was still in galley proof. Blotner identifies Faulkner's collaborator on "Revolt in the Earth" six years later as a Hollywood writer, but Dardis provides a fuller identification of this "somewhat legendary figure." [6]

According to Dardis, Dudley Murphy had contributed significantly to early, frequently experimental, films in Paris, New York, and Mexico, as well as in Hollywood. He was photographer, writer, producer, or director of both short and full-length films before collaborating on "Revolt in the Earth." It would seem that between Faulkner and Murphy there was more than enough talent to produce a workable film proposal.

In his account of Faulkner's Hollywood career, Dardis writes that Faulkner had known Dudley Murphy very briefly when they began their collaboration on "Revolt in the Earth." Perhaps the project brought them together for the first time; it is not clear.

Faulkner's inexperience with filmscript writing seems to have been taken for granted even by the film studios which

---

[6] Tom Dardis, *Some Time in the Sun* (Scribner's, 1976), 126–27. *The New York Times Directory of Film*, which lists film credits without comment, identifies Dudley Murphy as cinematographer of *The Soul of Cypress* (1921); director of *Confessions of a Co-Ed* (1931), *The Emperor Jones* (1933), *The Night is Young* (1935), *Don't Gamble with Love* (1936), *One Third of a Nation* (1939), and *Main Street Lawyer* (1939); as screenwriter of *One Third of a Nation*, Arthur Arent's stageplay.

Of these titles Dardis mentions only *The Emperor Jones*. He says Murphy was the producer as well as the director of this film (Eugene O'Neill's play, with Paul Robeson in the title role). He adds to the *Times* list, however, that Murphy was the photographer of Fernand Léger's short abstract film *Ballet Mécanique* (1924), that he directed the short film *St. Louis Blues* (1929), which was Bessie Smith's only film performance, and that he "had made" another short, *Black and Tan* (1933), with Duke Ellington.

62

employed him. He was always assigned a collaborator or two, and invariably he was the junior member of the partnership or team. For "Revolt in the Earth," says Dardis, Murphy acted as salesman or agent as well as collaborator, and the script circulated for some time and got "some nibbles, including a protracted one from Warner Brothers." This protracted nibble ended in Robert Buckner's note. Murphy's having given the script to Warner Brothers for their consideration would have made it easy for Buckner to pretend that Faulkner was not to blame for its quality or taste.

Although the proposed movie would have been offensive to many people and tasteless, Hollywood has produced and made money on equally unpromising material, and I do not think "Revolt in the Earth" should be excluded from the Sutpen continuum.

The note with which Robert Buckner rejected "Revolt in the Earth" was dated January 6, 1943, long after the publication of *Absalom, Absalom!* and "Wash." One of the fragmentary items of the Rowan Oak papers, however, indicates that the story on which the filmscript was based must have antedated the novel and even the Don-and-I stories. The single sheet contains a scrap of dialogue between Clytie and Wash, and for that reason the page was placed among early fragments of *Absalom, Absalom!* in the Jill Faulkner Summers Archive, but the dialogue contains several references that do not fit the novel and do fit the filmscript.

I believe the fragment was typed in 1925 or earlier. In the same collection or accumulation of manuscripts and typescripts is a typed copy of Faulkner's poem "The Faun," which was published in *The Double Dealer* in New Orleans in April 1925 (Faulkner and Spratling left New Orleans for Europe in

August of that year). The two sheets seem to have been typed on the same typewriter on the same kind of paper, and certainly they lay together untouched for a long time before they joined other pieces Faulkner gathered for work in the 1930s: the fragment of dialogue, the poem, and several other sheets in the collection have been nibbled by mice or insects, their top left corners rounded off by tiny teeth or other chewing equipment—that's what it looks like to me, anyway.

The Wash of the dialogue fragment complains to Clytie of his father's, Sutpen's, rejection of his mother, who lived long after the day of Wash's birth, long enough at least to instill in her growing child his only defense against the world, *hating*. This Wash also mentions the death of the grandfather for whom he was named—*that* Wash had killed himself by triggering a shotgun with his toe on the day of Wash's birth.[7] Short as it is, the dialogue manages to include references to other things which tie it to the filmscript instead of to the novel—a statue of Sutpen overgrown with subtropical vegetation, snakes, and a houseboat on the bayou.

Episodes from the lives of Thomas Sutpen and his family as related in *Absalom, Absalom!* and "Evangeline" are easily recognized in the melodramatic hodgepodge of "Revolt in the Earth," but they are touched lightly, minimized by distortion, and lost in digressions and extensions of the novel's plot. The main business of the film, if it had been produced, would have been the fulfillment of a curse pronounced in the beginning of the movie at the birth of Clytie, one of two illegitimate Sutpens born at about the same time:

[7] In the fragment, Wash is Sutpen's and Wash (Jones)'s grandson, but in the filmscript he is the great-grandson of both men. There, as in *Absalom, Absalom!*, it is important that Sutpen's last child be a girl.

> When de devil spawn on Sutpen land
> dey'll be a revolt in earth till
> Sutpen land has swallowed Sutpen birth.

Standing above the Negro mother in a cabin, Sutpen makes his impression on the audience with virtually the same statement that made Wash Jones kill him in "Wash" and *Absalom, Absalom!*: "Well, Sarah, they tell me you have brought me a heifer." He names the child Clytemnestra.

At the second birth, a white child born in a houseboat in the bayou, the father repeats his callous performance: "Well, Milly. Too bad its not a calf. . . . Too bad its not a boy. Then you could call him Wash, after his grandfather." (In the later fictions, Milly is Wash's granddaughter, not his daughter; it is *her* child who, by being born a girl, brings down the house of Sutpen.)

"Revolt in the Earth" would have moved very rapidly through the story that was so important to Quentin in the second half of *Absalom, Absalom!*. In short order Judith becomes engaged to Charles Bon, and Charles and Henry go together to New Orleans where Henry learns that Bon has a mulatto mistress and a child. Henry kills Bon. With hardly any beginning to the Civil War, Henry is killed in battle at his father's feet, and then Sutpen himself is killed on the battlefield.

Like Judith Shegog of Oxford, Mississippi, whose ghost was supposed to haunt the house Faulkner lived in and whose father, Colonal Robert Shegog, was—if anyone was—the historic figure on whom Colonel Thomas Sutpen was based, Judith Sutpen is wooed by a Yankee soldier; but unlike Judith Shegog, who broke her neck trying to descend a ladder in an elopement attempt, this Judith lives to marry her Yankee. In a Cleveland, Ohio, hospital for the birth of a child, Judith hears "drums" and bears a little girl. Clytie, meanwhile, has a child by a Negro soldier, and a third child, born to Milly's daughter, is bleakly dubbed "Wash Got-no-name."

After the birth of her child, Judith moves with her family to England. Photographs inscribed to Clytie appear in the old Sutpen house. The first is a portrait of Judith, now about seventy, as Clytie is, with her infant granddaughter Miriam. This is dated 1910. A later picture, that of a ten-year-old girl, is inscribed "To Clytie from Miriam."

Eventually Judith's granddaughter returns to Sutpen's plantation with a British clergyman husband to reestablish her family claim to the estate. The Englishman is naively fascinated by the Negroes living on the place, especially their religious activities. He is eager to observe and goes off excitedly into the swamp to witness a "baptism." Miriam's presence on Sutpen land stirs up a welter of voodoo drums, skulking Negroes and halfbreeds, murmured incantations, counter-voodoo, quicksand, and finally the snake slithering down a vine-hung statue of her great-grandfather.

Clytie and Wash (mulatto and poor white, they are Sutpen's daughter and his grandson) lead opposing forces of witchcraft. Wash, seeming to forget his own Sutpen blood, seeks fulfillment of the curse; Clytie tries to protect Miriam. Wash is a shadowy ominous figure who particularly gives Miriam the creeps and seems meant to do the same for the audience. The height of suspense is provided when having just saved Miriam from quicksand Wash fairly mesmerizes her in what could have been a fairly effective exchange:

66

WASH: You belong to this land. You folks do. You should know
how to find your way home.
MIRIAM: Do you belong to it, too?
WASH: No. It belongs to me.
MIRIAM: Belongs to you?
WASH: You folks left it. Now it belongs to me.
MIRIAM: Who are you?
WASH: Wash.

His psychic hold on Miriam established, Wash directs her out
of the swamp, but she is drawn out of the old mansion to his
cabin. Wash follows her in and closes the door.

Clytie, however, is alert to all this. She kills a piglet with a
butcher knife and performs an urgent ceremony with one of
its ribs, at least temporarily counteracting Wash's magic.

The clergyman comes tearing out of the swamp in fright,
Miriam rushes toward him, and they both blunder into the
quicksand, where they are swallowed up. Wash Got-no-name,
making a rescue attempt, drowns in the creek. Clytie survives. Then the snake is shown slithering down from the
statue and gliding out of sight in the undergrowth.

Reading "Revolt in the Earth," an admirer of *Absalom,
Absalom!* ponders *why* promiscuous miscegenation, voodoo,
cruelty, and curses fulfilled are acceptable and moving in one
context but cheap and silly in another, and how Faulkner
could have been even partially unaware of the difference—as
he must have been to have expected Buckner to read the
proposal.

The film plot is a strange combination of very early Sutpen
material and very late Sutpen material. Its own early scenes
could hardly have been conceived *after* Faulkner had worked

out, with Quentin, the Henry-Judith-Charles Bon story, much less the story of Thomas Sutpen's life from his boyhood to his death; yet the film action moves forward to the 1930s when Miriam, born in 1909 or 1910, is old enough to marry and bring her husband home across the Atlantic. And the writing of the script, although it bears no date but the date of its rejection (January 1943), must have been sometime after *Absalom, Absalom!* was published in 1936.

Faulkner might have given Dudley Murphy an old short story or script, the one from which a fragment of conversation between characters named Clytie and Wash survives, and asked him to see if it could be worked into a preliminary script for a movie. It is probably not possible any longer to determine how closely the two men actually worked on "Revolt in the Earth"; only guesses can be made from the strange document, the script of a justly unmade movie.

Even if we overlook the last part of "Revolt in the Earth," which is totally foreign to *Absalom, Absalom!*, the early scenes are pertinent to the growth and spread of the legends of Sutpen. Like "Evangeline" the filmscript is as important to the novel for what it does not include as for what it does. Sutpen's miscegenation with the mother of Clytie and his brutally unfeeling treatment of the poor white girl who is here Wash's daughter are the basic revelations of Sutpen's character and personality in this evidently primal Sutpen legend. Plantation owner or no, he is a brute, and his sole function in the plot is to establish the curse upon his land and all his descendants legitimate and illegitimate.

The story of Charles Bon and Sutpen's children Henry and Judith serves almost no purpose in "Revolt in the Earth," but even more significantly here than in "Evangeline" there is no suggestion that an alliance between Charles and Judith would have been incestuous. Henry's objection is to Bon's union with a New Orleans woman of mixed blood. The deaths of both Henry and his father during the Civil War preclude even the haunted house story of "Evangeline" and *Absalom, Absalom!*

Most important of all, the filmscript does without the narrators of the novel—Rosa Coldfield, Quentin's father, and all those Jeffersonians through whom Quentin has "always known" the Sutpen stories, and, of course, with Quentin himself and Shreve. Without their unifying force and emotional involvement, the stories of Sutpen fall away from each other into a scattering of unrelated episodes. Combined without the narrators, as in the filmscript, or taken separately, as in the Don-and-I stories, the legends of Sutpen are diminished to the level, or near it, of hackwork and cliché—as witness their rejection by editors and producers—with the single exception of "Wash." Clearly, the novel's narrators, especially its reluctant narrator, Quentin Compson, supply the larger dimension and cohesion that give life and credibility to *Absalom, Absalom!*

If this is Quentin's effect on the legends of Sutpen, that his interference with these old tales and telling raises them from tasteless and sometimes offensive trivia, unpublishable by the editorial standards of Faulkner's time, to the level of high art in a novel which has held the attention and the imaginations of readers and critics for four decades and is still going strong, such dynamic force must have a counterforce. What was the effect of the Sutpen stories on the youth who learned them and learned to tell them? This is the question Faulkner pursued in *Absalom, Absalom!*

The answer he found was layed out in the primary plot of the novel. There Quentin Compson, by inheritance and training a writer and a teller of tales, brings himself, Caddy's brother, to the point of no return on his path toward self-destruction.

Actually, the legends of Sutpen, as Quentin inherits them, have little to do with anything, even each other. But as he elaborates them, they have everything to do with Quentin. A developing fictionalist, apprentice to the mastercraftsman William Faulkner, Quentin forces unity upon the "ragtag and bob-ends of old tales and talking" by forcing them into the mold of his own experience.

Moving outward from the involved narrator, Quentin, to the controlling narrator, William Faulkner, it appears that the autobiographical aspects of Faulkner's dual character Quentin Compson are nebulous except for the facts that both Faulkner and Quentin were natives of northern Mississippi and approximate contemporaries. At least as a preserver and teller of tales, though, Quentin is obviously an avatar of his own creator; and if Quentin's fictive achievement in *Absalom, Absalom!* is remarkable, William Faulkner's is even more so. He has taken the same collection of unsuccessful fictions, added to them the dual Quentin, and forced the whole into a larger unifying mold to create his own masterpiece. "Maybe nothing ever happens once . . . but like ripples . . . ."

In 1923 Pablo Picasso had something to say about this. The Museum of Modern Art in New York used his statement in 1948 in a brochure introducing a series of exhibitions. Picasso said, "To me there is no past or future in art. . . . When I hear people speak of the evolution of an artist, it seems to me that they are considering him standing between two mirrors that face each other and reproduce his image an infinite number of times, and that they contemplate the successive images of one mirror as his past, and the images of the other mirror as his future. . . . They do not consider that they all are the same images in different planes."

V

Substance:
Historic Fact and Quentin's Fancy
in the Legends of Sutpen

Although *Absalom, Absalom!* occurs at an identifiable point in
the various continuums of Yoknapatawpha County, in the
legends of Sutpen, and in the "life" of Faulkner's dual
narrator-protagonist Quentin Compson, as well as in the writing career and in the life of William Faulkner, in the history
of Southern literature and of the South—and in the literature and history of increasingly wider areas until the ripples
meet in China or on the moon—the novel was offered as a self-
contained unit by its author and its publisher. It should be
analyzable without reference to anything outside itself.

Elimination of peripheral considerations would seem a
movement toward simplicity, but *Absalom, Absalom!* even
stripped bare is confusing. It has generated so many attempts
at plot analysis that it is time now to ask the next question:
why can not readers of this novel tell you at its end just what
happens in *Absalom, Absalom!* ? Why can they not with cer-
tainty list the events of the Sutpen legends either chronologically or unchronologically?

What are the facts about Thomas Sutpen and his heirs?
From whom does Quentin receive each of them and when?
What does happen in *Absalom, Absalom!*, sure enough? Even
Southern scholars have touched too lightly on that *sure*

enough. Its consideration, I believe, will reveal not only what happens but what does not, and also why attempts at ordering the chronology have been so inconclusive and so strewn with errors.

In September 1909, at the beginning of the novel, the citizens of Jefferson, Mississippi, know all they are ever to know about Thomas Sutpen, but Sutpen the legend is just coming into its own. The fictive process of its expansion is being helped mightily, though reluctantly, by young Quentin Compson, drafted to the hearing and telling by old Miss Rosa Coldfield.

Quentin is far from the first fictionalizer of the material. It has been modified and embellished and created anew by each of its narrators, nearly a dozen of them in the novel, not counting the Sutpen and other Negroes and the more-or-less uninvolved townspeople.

The narrators of *Absalom, Absalom!*, starting with Thomas Sutpen himself, include Ellen Coldfield Sutpen, Rosa Coldfield, Judith Sutpen, possibly Charles Bon, and three generations of Compsons. After these, who all have a good or fair claim to knowledge, come Quentin's Harvard roommate, Shreve, and the reader. The reader must be included because almost invariably he is as caught up in figuring out what must have happened as Shreve is. Another narrative voice is easy to overlook: it is that of the objective or impersonal author— Faulkner himself—who offers no information at all about Sutpen or his immediate family and only minimal stage directions for Quentin and his informants.

Even Wash Jones has a narrative function of sorts when he tells Rosa that "Henry has done shot that durn French feller. Kilt him dead as a beef." (AA, 133) The only character in the book who narrates nothing is Henry Sutpen. Henry speaks directly to Quentin, but he does not say much: "Henry Sutpen . . . Four years . . . To die, Yes . . . Yes, to die . . . Four years . . . Henry Sutpen." (AA, 373)

All the Sutpen legends in Absalom, Absalom! are reported as oral narrative, but the novel also includes two letters. One is Charles Bon's strange letter to Judith, a wan but vivid account of life in a retreating and nearly decimated army. The other is Mr. Compson's letter to Quentin reporting Miss Rosa's death and burial.

As in most frame stories, the Sutpen tales in Absalom, Absalom! are well told and fascinating, but they are ghost stories, while their tellers are flesh and blood. The living Rosa Coldfield's "female old flesh long embattled in virginity" sits before Quentin wearing lace and black silk, and its "rank smell" reaches him through the dust motes in evidence of her reality. (AA,8) But Rosa the sneaky little eavesdropper of four and Rosa the fourteen-year-old old maid are phantoms. As Rosa calls up her young self and the other phantoms, they are vivid to Quentin's mind's eye, "more true than truth" even, but vividness is not the criterion of hard fact. Indeed, for Quentin in this novel it is almost invariably the other way around. Visualizing Sutpen's tombstones, which he has actually seen in the Sutpen graveyard, as they follow the regiment through Virginia and home to Mississippi, Quentin thinks to himself, "No. If I had been there I could not have seen it this plain." (AA, 190)

The narration of any tale is so crucial to its credibility and memorability that it is not hard to believe that the high praise heaped upon Absalom, Absalom! is earned, in large part, by

Historic Fact and Quentin's Fancy in the Legends of Sutpen

Faulkner's careful selection and delineation of his narrators. That he meant for Quentin to take over the story of Thomas Sutpen in more ways than one seems clear when the novel is analyzed in terms of the comparative reality of its narrator-characters, especially Sutpen and Quentin. Quentin, who trod down his own shadow in *The Sound and the Fury*, is solid enough to cast that shadow. There is no mention anywhere of Sutpen's shadow. He is presented from the first pages of the novel *as* a shadow, a shade.

Another means of discerning the difference between fact and fancy in *Absalom, Absalom!* lies among the many discrepancies or seeming miscalculations in the Sutpen chronology. Four decades after the publication of the novel there is no published chronology in which errors are not demonstrable, some of them startling, as when one writer indicates in both his text and a time chart that Henry Sutpen, not Charles Bon, died in 1865,[1] or when in an early draft of my own study I fell to using the name Eulalia for Charles Bon's paramour.

The many critical attempts to establish the facts and the sequence of Sutpen chronology devolve from, and their errors are partially explainable by, the mistaken premises, first, that *Absalom, Absalom!* is primarily Sutpen's story, and second, that the events of the Sutpen story are supposed to have happened. Even in terms of the text, not to say the author's intent, most of them either did not happen or cannot be proved to have happened. The events that were real, again in terms of the text, are few, and for most of these there is some measure of substantiation. The unknown quantities are con-

[1] Joseph W. Reed, Jr., *Faulkner's Narrative* (New Haven and London: Yale University Press), 1973.

jectured by Quentin Compson and by his roommate Shreve. Shreve is not even very good at conjecture in this case because he is ignorant of the South and of Southerners.

Errors in the chronologies are further explainable by the extraordinary amount of repetition in the novel, the same incident being told by several narrators from varying distances and with a varying number of intermediaries to the telling. For instance, Rosa's offer to teach her niece, four years older than Rosa, such household arts as Rosa has somehow taught herself was related "with shrieks of amusement" by Rosa's sister Ellen to Grandmother Compson, who told her husband, who told their son (Grandmother Compson told him, too) who told Quentin, who tells Shreve, who repeats it with flourishes. What is more, most of these narrators have told the story many times to anyone who would listen. Rosa's offer of housekeeping lessons was one of the bits of lore in which Jason Compson's and his son Quentin's youths were steeped.

Errors are rendered inevitable by the fact that Quentin himself, like the other narrators, had trouble with the chronology, as did Faulkner *him*self. Climaxing the confusion, the chronology and genealogy Faulkner devised were put together hastily after the manuscript of the novel had been in the editors' hands for some time. The novel was intended to stand without these crutches, and neither should be considered part of the book.

The most obvious evidence of the haste with which Faulkner prepared his chronology is that the last two items, the finding of Henry Sutpen and Rosa's ill-starred errand to rescue him, are listed as having occurred in September and December of 1910 instead of in 1909. (One chronologist says

Quentin accompanied Rosa on both occasions,[2] but he did so only once.)

Faulkner made other errors of time calculation within the text itself. For example, he calls the interval between September and January five months. For another example, although the discrepancy may strike a more ruminative reader, Faulkner has none of the narrators remark the odd circumstance that although Ellen Coldfield's mother was alive when Ellen married Thomas Sutpen (Mrs. Coldfield died seven years later at Rosa's birth), it was Ellen's paternal aunt who "engineered" the elaborate wedding and tried to enforce attendance by those on the long guest list. Furthermore, the bride's mother did not attend the wedding—it was Ellen and her aunt whom Sutpen sheltered from the crowd.

Here is other evidence of careless ratiocination on Faulkner's part: Quentin, an oldest child, was born in 1891; his grandparents were married shortly before the Sutpen wedding (1834), and although it was evidently several years before the birth of their son, Quentin's father, either that son would have to have been the child of his parents' late middle age or Quentin would have to have been the child of *his* parents' late middle age (with his sister and brothers born even later), yet neither circumstance is hinted. It would be chronologically more appropriate for Sutpen's friend to have been Quentin's great-grandfather than his grandfather.

These discrepancies are unimportant to the unity of the novel, and, besides, they are typical of Faulkner's narrative

---

[2] C. Hugh Holman, "*Absalom, Absalom!* The Historian as Detective," *The Roots of Southern Writing: Essays on the Literature of the South* (Athens: University of Georgia Press, 1972), 171.

habits and the authorial privileges he insisted upon. Continuity and consistency from novel to novel throughout Faulkner's career were notoriously hit or miss. In *Absalom, Absalom!*, for instance, the Negro youth who accompanies Quentin and his father on the hunting excursion is Luster, but in *The Sound and the Fury* Luster is the contemporary of Quentin's niece, Caddy's daughter, who has not even been conceived by the end of *Absalom, Absalom!* This makes it impossible to date the hunting trip or to know how old Quentin was when (on the trip) he realized that Judith had paid for Charles Bon's tombstone and Clytie had somehow paid for Judith's.

Although it is now known that Faulkner chose Quentin to be the chief narrator in *Absalom, Absalom!* "because it is just before he is to commit suicide because of his sister," [3] Faulkner altered the very weather of late summer, 1909, between Quentin's two novels. In August Caddy introduced Quentin to Dalton Ames in a drizzling rain, but when Quentin accompanies Rosa through the hot dusty night to Sutpen's Hundred about a month later it has not rained for sixty days.

Although the ordering of events in *Absalom, Absalom!* (at least in Sutpen matters) is imprecise, the ordering of events in *The Sound and the Fury* is not. Those events are identifiable by the names of Benjy's successive attendants, the names of horses and ponies owned by the Compsons, and other similar devices which mark passing time. By these convenient tags the reader can order the scrambled memories of even the mindless Benjy and the distraught Quentin. Everything falls into sequence, the successive sections of the novel corroborating each other.

[3] William Faulkner to Harrison Smith, undated letter, Jill Faulkner Summers Archive.

Historic Fact and Quentin's Fancy in the Legends of Sutpen

From *The Sound and the Fury*, then, the great critical ordering game must have carried over to *Absalom, Absalom!* by sheer momentum. In *Absalom, Absalom!*, however, the distinction between the reality of the present and the lost reality of the past, one of the chief themes of the novel, obviates the necessity and even the usefulness of chronological precision in the Sutpen story.

That Faulkner did not clear up certain ambiguities about Sutpen and his family is true. That he *failed* to do so, as some have claimed,[4] is not true if he did not try. That he was unable to do so, as has been charged,[5] is at least unlikely, for the discrepancies serve a useful purpose—to distinguish between the Sutpen material and the Quentin material, between the unknowable past and the observable present.

The Quentin part of *Absalom, Absalom!* is left in no doubt whatever and contains no miscalculations except the count of months between September and January (Faulkner must have ticked it off on his fingers, counting both the first and the last named months).

Of course, Quentin is a fictional character as much as Sutpen is—or almost as much. Faulkner invented them both. But the interpretive discussion of fiction must begin with axioms as surely as a geometry problem must. The willing suspension of disbelief must begin somewhere, and in this case it must end somewhere. The axiom is that the frame is solid; the characters who speak and act in September 1909 and January 1910 existed. If you had been in Jefferson, Mississippi, or in Cambridge, Massachusetts, you could have

[4] See Walter J. Slatoff, *Quest for Failure: A Study of William Faulkner* (Ithaca: Cornell University Press, 1960).
[5] *Ibid.*

reached out and touched Quentin Compson, whose sister Caddy surrendered (gladly) her honor, and who could not bring himself to kill her lover, but who did (will) kill himself. Shortly after his confrontation with Caddy's lover, Dalton Ames, Quentin reluctantly considers the intertwined stories of Thomas Sutpen, his wife, his children, his father-in-law, his daughter's fiance, his sister-in-law, and his friend, Quentin's grandfather. In these stories Quentin sees himself and Caddy as Henry and Judith Sutpen and Dalton Ames as Charles Bon. Faulkner's novel is about the fictive process itself, and Quentin is the narrator-protagonist.

Here are several of the primary suppositions with which scholars have been working as with known facts, and here also are their contradictions carefully provided by Faulkner in the text of *Absalom, Absalom!* Here, too, are suggested alternatives, offered not as serious correction but to show the insubstantiality of the generally accepted fictions:

First, *Charles Bon was the son of Thomas Sutpen, born in Haiti.* This is Quentin's idea, inspired by his father's remarks that Henry Sutpen was to blame for his sister's "seduction" because Henry saw Charles Bon as a model and felt for him the admiration and love he would have felt for an older brother, and that Henry and Judith Sutpen were closer in physical and psychological make-up than even brother and sister could be expected to be. The parallels of these three—Henry, Judith, and Charles Bon—to himself, Caddy, and Dalton Ames were not to be avoided by Quentin, or for that matter, by his father. What is more, nowhere in the multiple telling of Sutpen's story by those who could know is there evidence that even Sutpen thought Bon his son. There is not the slightest suggestion that Charles Bon looked, acted, or felt akin to the darkly passionate and determined Sutpen blood which showed itself, even to the child eyes of four-year-old Rosa Coldfield, in Judith, Henry, and Clytie.

If the information Judith caused to be chiselled onto Bon's gravestone was not her subterfuge or someone else's, Charles Bon was born in New Orleans in December 1831. (*AA*, 190) If these data were misrepresented *to* Judith, her source of misinformation certainly belongs in the novel, as does the motivation for it, but it is not there. Indeed, when Henry met Bon at the University of Mississippi in 1859 a part of Bon's worldly glamour was his lack of any family. He had "for background the shadowy figure of a legal guardian rather than any parents." (*AA*, 74)

Second, Thomas Sutpen disclaimed his first wife and their child *because he learned that she had Negro blood.* That he disclaimed them Sutpen told Quentin's grandfather, but he did not say or suggest that they were part Negro. Nor did he say the child was Charles Bon. Sutpen, in General Compson's office in the last year of the Civil War, when he had brought to Jefferson the imported marble stones for Ellen's and his own graves, told the general—as Quentin relates it to Shreve—"how he had put his first wife aside like eleventh- and twelfth-century kings did: 'I found that she was not and could never be, through no fault of her own, adjunctive or incremental to the design which I had in mind, so I provided for her and put her aside.' " (*AA*, 240)

Cleanth Brooks has taken exception to the general unqualified belief that the first Mrs. Thomas Sutpen had Negro blood. He suggests two alternative possible reasons for her husband's putting her aside: she might not have been a virgin when Sutpen married her; she might even have been preg-

nant by another man (in which case her child, even if it were
Charles Bon, would not have been Sutpen's heir). Either of
these would certainly have seemed to Sutpen justification for
divorce—legal or *de facto*. Professor Brooks points out that
"nineteenth century literature is full of stories of rejection for
such cause." [6] In fact, the situation is not unknown in
twentieth-century literature: a case very much in point—
Caddy Compson Head in *The Sound and the Fury*.

Another possible explanation would be inheritable or sup-
posedly inheritable mental deficiency—the woman or her
child or both might actually have become insane. If this had
been the woman's flaw, and if she *was* the mother of Charles
Bon, it would account for the idiocy of Bon's grandson. (Although Jim Bond's mother is said to have been "ape-like" and
mentally sluggish, she is not said to have been idiotic.) Maybe
Eulalia Sutpen was illiterate and disinclined to remedy the
fault.

Still another possibility is this: the young Haitian woman of
Spanish descent might have been embarrassingly over-sexed
for a socially ambitious man like Sutpen, or maybe she had
fits.

The supposed Negro blood of Sutpen's first wife (strangely,
in the South) did not occur to Quentin's father during the
many years of his familiarity with the legends of Sutpen. Nor
had it occurred to his father, the general, or the idea would
almost certainly have been passed on—there is no evidence of
reluctance on General Compson's part to air everything he
knew or suspected of his friend's affairs. Nor does it seem to

[6] Cleanth Brooks, "The Secret of Bon's Parentage," Part I of "On *Absalom,
Absalom!*" *MOSAIC VII/1*, ed. James B. Meriwether (Winnipeg: University
of Manitoba Press, 1973).

have occurred to any of Jefferson's other citizens between
1831 and 1909.

Professor Brooks's comments on this topic are partially in
answer to Floyd Watkins's article "What Happens in *Absalom, Absalom!*?" but more directly to Gerald Langford's introduction to his book collating the Texas manuscript with the
published novel.[7] Both Watkins and Langford have assumed
that General Compson believed Sutpen deliberately implied,
when he said he had been told she was Spanish, that his first
wife's dark complexion and hair were actually not Spanish but
negroid. Langford's study indicates that in an early draft Mr.
Compson and others *knew* Bon to be both Negro and Sutpen,
but Langford does not comment on the significance of Faulkner's having changed this. That Faulkner called on Quentin to
invent these "facts" at one blow demotes Sutpen and pro-
motes Quentin to star billing in the cast of *Absalom, Absalom!,* for it moves the novel's arena of conflict from Sutpen's
to Quentin's mind.

Third, it seems generally taken for granted that *Mr. Compson's "realization" of the woman's (and Charles Bon's) Negro
blood is based on something Quentin learned from Henry Sutpen.* It is plain enough that this is something Quentin told his
father the morning after he met Henry. Quentin tells Shreve
that it was he who gave his father this information, but Quentin does not claim that Henry told him *anything* except his
name and that he had come home four years earlier to die. It
is Quentin who jumped to the conclusion or invented "just

---

[7] Floyd Watkins, "What Happens in *Absalom, Absalom!*?," *Modern Fiction
Studies*, 13 (Spring 1967), 79–87; Gerald Langford, *Faulkner's Revision of
Absalom, Absalom!: A Collation of the Manuscript and the Published Book*
(Austin: University of Texas Press, 1971).

anything" when he needed an explanation more acceptable to himself than incest (which he also invented) for the murder of Charles Bon.

Where would Quentin have found such an idea? Quentin was a literate young man, and, as Professor Brooks points out, Southern fiction abounds in miscegenation discovered "too late." The subject occurs so often and so simplistically that by Faulkner's time it was almost too "tacky" for serious use. I believe Faulkner meant it, in *Absalom, Absalom!*, to be recognizable as the ready-at-hand unanswerable-though-false "reason" with which Quentin attempts to stop the painful bombardment of his father's effort to imagine *why* Sutpen forbade Judith's marriage and *why* Henry killed Charles Bon.

In the stories where Quentin could have found this "answer," the taint is usually in the heritage of a lovely young woman who is herself unaware of it. After a fairy-tale romance and wedding, sometimes after the birth of a dark-skinned child with strangely shaped features, the secret is out, and the genteel rich adoring husband has no course but to renounce. Then there is usually a suicide or two, and the poignant tragedy closes with revelation of a mistake: she did not have Negro blood, after all. In "Desiree's Baby," Kate Chopin's classic use of the theme, the child's father discovers that it is *he* whose blood is tainted.

Even Mark Twain included an incidence of this literary phenomenon in a story, but there (in "The Man That Corrupted Hadleyburg") the reference is fleeting and the intent is satiric. Hadleyburg's only genuinely good man had had a tragic love affair, his sweetheart having died before their wedding, and "soon after the girl's death the village found out, or thought it found out, that she carried a spoonful of Negro

blood in her veins." Twain here uses the Negro taint in exactly the same way Quentin uses it—to put an end to the
search for unobtainable information, to pose an unques-
tionable solution to an insoluble question.

Although Quentin himself implied to Shreve and seems to
have implied to his father that he had learned from Henry
that Bon was part Negro, what we know of their meeting fails
to support such an implication.

The impact on Quentin of his meeting with Henry is revealed in Faulkner's—not Quentin's—much-delayed account
of it and in the reaction Quentin remembers—that he rushed
home in a kind of frenzy and fell sweating and half-dressed
upon his bed, where waking or sleeping he lived over and
over the confrontation. Quentin's memory of his meeting with
Henry Sutpen, which Faulkner withholds until the end of the
novel, seems complete in the minutest detail, as traumatic experiences do, but there is no mention in it of Charles Bon or
of his murder.

Quentin's conversation with Henry not only seems complete and accurate, it is also plausibly complete and accurate.
Calm or frightened, Quentin was not likely to have launched
a cub-reporter-style interview with Henry Sutpen in the circumstances of their meeting, and Henry was even less likely
to have told all, asked or not, to a young stranger who burst
into his death chamber only a few seconds after a demoniac
little old lady who may or may not have introduced herself to
Henry as his Aunt Rosa before she bolted wild-eyed out
again. In view of his advanced age and his admitted expecta-
tion of death, Henry measured up to the occasion admirably
by stating his name and his reason for being there.

What is more, there is no time allowed in Quentin's memory of the meeting for more talk than the reported brief conversation. As Rosa passed him on the stair Clytie had directed Jim Bond, in Quentin's hearing, to see Rosa to the buggy at the end of the drive. Rosa, in her excitement, moves very fast for a frail woman of sixty-four, but Quentin is close behind her and her escort on the dark pathway. Although he has traversed the long upstairs hallway, conducted his circular exchange with Henry, and returned through the hallway and down the stairs to leave the house, he is close enough on Rosa's heels to hear her words to Jim Bond and her stumbling and falling.

No, Quentin did not learn anything from Henry Sutpen except that the man was real, that a character from a fantasy had, and had always had, corporeal reality, and by extension that a young man very much like himself and in circumstances similar to his had had the nerve to kill his sister's sweetheart.

One of the remarks Quentin hears Miss Rosa address to Jim Bond, elsewhere in this novel presumed to be the great-grandson of Thomas Sutpen, seems flatly to deny that presumption. When she falls in the dark, Rosa demands that he help her to her feet. "Help me up! You aint any Sutpen! You dont have to leave me lying in the dirt!" (AA, 371) Even if "You aint any Sutpen!" indicates only that his being of Sutpen descent has never occurred to Rosa, it is a flat denial by one who was much closer to the facts than Quentin was. However, it is not, like Quentin's denials, overdone, hence self-negating.

There is something else to be explained about this episode: it also concerns Jim Bond. Before Quentin meets Henry, from whom he claims to have learned of Bon's being part Negro, Quentin has *already* decided that Bon was Sutpen's son, for he looks over his shoulder as he ascends the stairway and, seeing Bon's idiot grandson, who is known to have been more than half black (his paternal grandmother was an octoroon, and his mother was a full-blooded Negress), he identifies Jim Bond as "the scion, the heir, the apparent (though not obvious)," (*AA*, 370) although whatever Jim Bond is heir to he has inherited through his grandfather, Charles Bon—not from the Sutpens. Judith did not legally adopt Jim Bond's father, Charles Etienne Saint-Valery Bon; she did not even clarify for anyone in Jefferson whether this child of Charles Bon and the octoroon called her Miss Judith, Aunt Judith, or something else.

A fourth important misconception about *Absalom, Absalom!* is that Quentin is sincere in the ratiocination through which he leads Shreve: *he believes his own fantasy of incest and miscegenation.* On the contrary, Quentin knows that he is projecting Caddy's affair with Dalton Ames and his own jealous despair onto the young Sutpens and Charles Bon.

Faulkner has included in the dormitory sequences of *Absalom, Absalom!* a powerful analogue of the Apostle Peter's denial of Christ. In fact, he almost carries it too far, for it is in the midst of Shreve's frequent exclamation, "Jesus!" Three times Quentin denies that he knows how a young man might feel about incestuous love. As Peter's denials follow midnight and begin with the King James version of "I don't know what you are talking about," so do Quentin's begin after midnight and deny knowledge. The surprise is that the third denial is not immediately followed by the crowing of a cock (as, indeed, it is if you want to consider Shreve cocky or cocksure).

Shreve is trying to imagine the temptation of Charles Bon with Judith set before him like a dish of sherbet to be enjoyed for the simple taking, all in the lush setting of Mississippi springtime as Quentin himself has described it to Shreve. In the midst of Shreve's speech Faulkner supplies him with the name of Christ's betrayer, and a little later supplies the objective narrator with the word *tomb*:

> . . . that country where he had never spent a spring before and you said North Mississippi is a little harder country than Louisiana, with dogwood and violets and the early scentless flowers but the earth and the nights still a little cold and the hard tight sticky buds like young girls' nipples on alder and Judas trees and beech and maple and even something young in the cedars like he never saw before . . . .

Having spread this sensuous evocation of Quentin's homeland before his friend, Shreve makes it even worse: "And who to say if it wasn't maybe the possibility of incest [the roommates have long-since accepted the idea that Bon is Judith's half-brother], because who (without a sister; I don't know about the others) has been in love and not discovered the vain evanescence of the fleshly encounter." (AA, 323)

Evidently Shreve does not have a sister, but Quentin does, though she has not been mentioned in *Absalom, Absalom!*, so Quentin is one of the "others" Shreve does not know about. For Quentin, in *The Sound and the Fury*, every man belonged to one of these two categories, those who have sisters and those who do not, the first frantically jealous of their sisters' virginity, and the second callously convinced that "they're all bitches."

> . . . the vain evanescence of the fleshly encounter: who has not had to realize that when the brief all is done you must retreat from both love and pleasure, gather up your own rubbish and refuse—the hats and pants and shoes which you drag through the

world—and retreat since the gods condone and practice these and the dreamy immeasurable coupling which floats oblivious above the trammeling and harried instant, the: *was-not, is: was:* (*AA*, 323–24)

The echoes of *The Sound and the Fury* are loud and clear. Quentin cannot miss them. They are practically his own thought-words from the earlier novel. Shreve hammers on relentlessly:

". . . but maybe if there were sin too maybe you would not be permitted to escape, uncouple, return—Aint that right?" He ceased, he could have been interrupted easily now. Quentin could have spoke now, but Quentin did not. He just sat as before, his hands in his trousers pockets, his shoulders hugged inward and hunched, his face lowered and he looked somehow curiously smaller than he actually was . . . . (*AA*, 324)

In August 1909, with Caddy's virginity a thing of the past, Quentin had tried illogically to convince her that it was *he* who had been her lover. He would kill them both and retreat with Caddy to hell.

"Because if it were just a hell beyond that: the clean flame the two of us more than dead. Then you will have only me then only me then the two of us amid the pointing and the horror beyond the clean flame. . . . Only you and me then amid the pointing and the horror walled by the clean flame . . . ." (*SF*, 144)

After Shreve's "Aint that right?" there is a pause into which these profoundly morbid meditations would fit very nicely. Then, although he knows what Shreve means much better than Shreve can imagine,

"I dont know," Quentin said.
"All right," Shreve said. "Maybe I dont either. Only, Jesus, someday you are bound to fall in love. They just wouldn't beat

you that way. It would be like God had got Jesus born and saw that he had the carpenter tools and then never gave him anything to build with them. Dont you believe that?"

Quentin's reply is his second denial:

"I dont know," Quentin said. He did not move. Shreve looked at him. Even while they were not talking their breath in the tomblike air vaporized gently and quietly. The chimes for midnight would have rung some time ago now.
"You mean, it dont matter to you?"

In the Biblical parallel to this inquisition, Peter's speech (his Galilean accent) betrays him and his questioner tells him so. In *Absalom, Absalom!* Shreve spares Quentin the necessity of speaking, but he lets Quentin know that he is not fooled: " 'That's right. Dont say it. Because I would know you were lying—All right then. Listen . . . .' " (*AA*, 324–25)

Like Quentin's denial at the end of the novel that he hates the South, this triple denial of his obsession is anything but convincing either to Shreve or to readers who followed Quentin to his death in *The Sound and the Fury*.

I shall question only one more questionable matter in *Absalom, Absalom!*, although this does not exhaust the list. Faulkner withheld or failed to create many things for which he provided places in this novel. Elsewhere marvelously inventive, he offers here only puzzles for which Quentin must find the answers. Faulkner, the master story-teller, sets up the telling for his favorite apprentice. As though to offer Quentin the opportunity his suicide almost precluded, Faulkner handed him "Evangeline" to see what Quentin could do with it; or so, at least, it seems, for the author does not intervene at all in Quentin's shaping of that unpublished short story into his own self-portrait.

The most obviously deliberate omissions in Faulkner's novel are the salutation and signature by which the letter Mr. Compson shows Quentin could have been identified. Quentin is told, and he believes, that *the letter was written by Charles Bon to Judith Sutpen,* but was it? Why are there no salutation and no signature, no name or other identifiable reference to person or place in the body of the letter, no endearment? There are only pronouns: " 'You will notice how I insult neither of us by claiming . . . . We have waited long enough.' "

There is the stand-off-ish refusal to make any emotional intrusion: " 'I insult neither of us . . . . You will notice how I do not insult you either by saying I have waited long enough . . . therefore . . . I do not add, expect me. Because I cannot say when to expect me.' " (*AA*, 131)

Strangest of all is the morose ending (if it is the ending of the letter): " '. . . I now believe that you and I are, strangely enough, included among those doomed to live.' " (*AA*, 132) It does not sound like something even a war-weary gentleman would write to his fiancee. It does, though, have the ring of something a man might write to his wife, to a woman with whom he had been through one or more periods of heartache.

If Charles Bon wrote this not-begun and not-ended letter, might he have written it not to Judith but to the octoroon mother of his son, the woman whom Faulkner failed to name even in the chronology appended to the novel? If such a letter had somehow come into Henry's hands, might Henry have killed Bon because Bon evidently intended to continue his liaison with the octoroon whether he married Judith or not? Perhaps—no conjecture can match Quentin's—Henry shot Charles Bon over a gambling debt. Or perhaps the pistol went off accidentally. Maybe Bon meant to break his engagement and Henry would not permit that.

The point is that we do not know, because Quentin did not know. Even Faulkner did not feel obliged to figure out the irretrievable past but stopped with "probably" and "perhaps"—and even behind these shields, his "probably" and "perhaps," he hedged his bets in contradiction. Near the close of the novel he says that Quentin and Shreve were "probably right" about the elements of the story which they conjectured, but at the height of their inventiveness he had described their creations as people and events that "perhaps had never existed at all anywhere." Meanwhile, with elaborate detail and great skill he devoted his effort in *Absalom, Absalom!* to fitting the story of Sutpen's heirs to the already established story of Quentin Compson, because Quentin could tell it in no other terms.

VI

The Picture Plane:
Controlling Images in *Absalom, Absalom!*

Quentin Compson's imagination is strongly visual, and the things he sees or seems to see throughout the long listening forced upon him in *Absalom, Absalom!* are pictures. Their picture quality is explicit—static or nearly so, two-dimensional. Faulkner describes them as if they were framed, hung on a wall or resting on an easel or shown on a silvered screen. Quentin sits before them and observes. Though his senses are engaged, he is physically outside or beyond the pictures conjured up by Rosa or his father, but each of the important ones is overlaid on a traumatic moment, a confrontation, which Quentin experienced in *The Sound and the Fury*.

Faulkner has placed one or two of these controlling mental pictures at the climax of each of the chapters in the first half of *Absalom, Absalom!*, where Quentin is amassing the information about the Sutpen family from which he and Shreve, in the last chapters of the novel, will construct their romantic epic of Sutpen's heirs.

The controlling images are always reminiscent of *The Sound and the Fury* and invariably they pull the reader's attention away from Thomas Sutpen and his family, directing it back to the earlier novel. Key scenes from the stories of Sutpen are visualized by Quentin like stills or brief clips from a movie in which he, Caddy, and Dalton Ames have played the parts of Henry and Judith Sutpen and Charles Bon.

One of these "frozen moments" is "planted" somewhere in the course of each chapter. Near the end of the chapter it is repeated. The reader is told that Quentin has not been listening to Rosa or his father, that he has been "caught" on the imagined scene. The Sutpen material just narrated becomes unimportant and the novel turns back to Quentin and to *The Sound and the Fury*.

Throughout the work, these strategically placed images are supported by and interwoven with more subtle, somewhat less arresting imagery also evoking the earlier novel. On the first page of *Absalom, Absalom!*, for instance, Quentin sits facing the window of Miss Rosa Coldfield's "office" in Jefferson, just as in his section of *The Sound and the Fury* he wakes facing the window of his dormitory room in Cambridge. In each case the changing angle of light is a reminder of the passing of time and also of its intransigence. In the earlier novel, Quentin's section begins: "When the shadow of the sash appeared on the curtains it was between seven and eight oclock and then I was in time again, hearing the watch." (*SF*, 93) In *Absalom, Absalom!*, Quentin sits in Rosa Coldfield's house, "the blinds all closed and fastened . . . and [the room] (as the sun shone fuller and fuller on that side of the house) became latticed with yellow slashes full of dust motes which Quentin thought of as being flecks of the dead old paint itself blown inward from the scaling blinds as wind might have blown them." (*AA*, 7)

The author's deliberate ambiguity in *Absalom, Absalom!* compounds the danger of reading things into its imagery. At the same time, paradoxically, this reading-in seems to be just what Faulkner wanted from his readers. The danger of misreading-in is implicit. Neither Quentin's sister nor his suicide is mentioned in *Absalom, Absalom!* but they are both so important to the novel—and the imagery is so dependent upon awareness of them—Faulkner must have assumed that his readers would know the earlier novel and that the images would be as evocative for them as for Quentin.

The images do, indeed, control Quentin's and Shreve's fictionalizing. *Absalom, Absalom!* itself is a demonstration of the process by which a complicated story can be derived from an inadequate set of facts if those facts are reinforced by vivid imagery. In it Faulkner has shown, as he did in *The Sound and the Fury*, how to build a novel from mental pictures.

There are two sets of evocative images in *Absalom, Absalom!*: those by which Quentin identifies himself, Caddy, and Dalton Ames with Henry Sutpen, Judith Sutpen, and Charles Bon, and those by which only the reader is reminded of *The Sound and the Fury*. The first control Quentin's involvement with the Sutpen story. The second lend richness through dramatic irony to the later novel. The ironic images join the two stories, Quentin's and Sutpen's, at points which Quentin would not have "caught" because his suicide comes too early in *The Sound and the Fury* or because *Absalom, Absalom!* "occurs" before Caddy's engagement and wedding. They are strong evidence that Faulkner deliberately held one novel in mind while writing the other one. The other images—those Quentin "cannot pass"—control his development of the Sutpen narrative and prove that Quentin held the summer of 1909 obsessively in mind while Rosa and his father led him through their review and extension of the Sutpen legends, unwittingly pointing for him the direction on which he would carry them. The ironic images occur throughout the novel but belong more importantly to the second half of *Absalom, Absalom!* The controlling images are important throughout but have more dramatic weight in the first five chapters.

The first of the controlling images is placed at the climax of the first chapter, as subsequent controlling images will be placed at the climaxes of Chapters II, III, IV, and V. It is precisely the image from which Faulkner developed *The Sound and the Fury*: a spunky little girl, having climbed to a forbidden place, looks down unafraid at an adult ritual which is essentially cruel—in a way usurping a boy's place at a rite of passage.

In *Absalom, Absalom!* the scene is Sutpen's stable. Ellen Sutpen (Rosa is telling Quentin) misses her children; she runs to the barn where she knows her husband to be engaged in a brutal boxing match with one of his slaves before an audience of his drinking and hunting cronies and other slaves; she finds that Sutpen has forced Henry to watch (Henry is fourteen years old) and that Henry has been terrified into hysterical nausea by the sight. Ellen suspects that Judith (aged twelve) has also been exposed to the degrading spectacle, but Sutpen denies it (the punctuation is Faulkner's—Rosa, speaking to Quentin, quotes Ellen and Thomas Sutpen):

> " 'I wish I could believe you,' Ellen said. 'I want to believe you.' Then she began to call. 'Judith!' she called in a voice calm and sweet and filled with despair: 'Judith honey! Time to come to bed.'
>
> "But I was not there [Rosa tells Quentin] I was not there to see the two Sutpen faces this time—once on Judith and once on the negro girl beside her—looking down through the square entrance to the loft." (*AA*, 30)

In *The Sound and the Fury* the scene was the yard of the Compson's house on the day of "Damuddy's" funeral. Caddy has muddied her clothes playing in the creek so that when she climbs up into a peartree to look through the window at the funeral—which all but Quentin believe is an adult party— her brothers and the Compson Negroes, looking up, see the soiled seat of her drawers in the twilight in the blossoming tree.

In *Absalom, Absalom!* Rosa's description of Judith in the loft and Henry's hysteria is the beginning of Quentin's iden- tification of himself with Henry Sutpen. The image of Judith (with Clytie) looking down, solemn but unafraid, is so like Caddy in the peartree looking through the window at her grandmother's funeral that Quentin cannot fail to extend his self-identification with Henry to his identification of Caddy with Henry's sister.

The second chapter of *Absalom, Absalom!* brings Quentin home from his visit to Rosa. After supper he has a long talk with his father on the front gallery of the Compson house. Mr. Compson takes over from Rosa as narrator and supplies, from the viewpoint of the townsfolk in general, and of General Compson (Quentin's grandfather) in particular, a more humane and admiring account of Thomas Sutpen in the early years of his life in Jefferson than Rosa could manage.

The setting of this chapter again suggests *The Sound and the Fury*. In August 1909 (in *The Sound and the Fury*) this same father and son sat in the evening on the same gallery and talked about honor, Southern women, incest, and sui- cide—the same topics they discuss now in September of the same year. Quentin's ordeal by fragrance during Caddy's affair with Dalton Ames is suggested by the opening lines of the

chapter: "It was a summer of wistaria. The twilight was full of
it and of the smell of his father's cigar as they sat on the front
gallery after supper . . . ." (*AA*, 31)

Aside from the world *twilight*, which was the original title
of the story that grew into *The Sound and the Fury*, and the
porch setting, the wistaria, already mentioned in the first
chapter of *Absalom, Absalom!*, recalls this and other passages
of Quentin's tangled thought-flow on the day of his suicide:

> Honeysuckle was the saddest odour of all, I think. I remember
> lots of them. Wistaria was one . . . . When it bloomed in the
> spring and it rained the smell was everywhere you didn't notice it
> so much at other times but when it rained the smell began to
> come into the house at twilight either it would rain more at twi-
> light or there was something in the light itself but it always
> smelled strongest then I would lie in bed thinking when will it
> stop when will it stop. . . . Sometimes I could put myself to
> sleep saying that over and over until the honeysuckle got all
> mixed up in it the whole thing came to symbolize night and
> unrest. (*SF*, 210–11)

Chapter II of *Absalom, Absalom!*, like Chapter I, builds to
a dramatic ending, and again the climactic scene is suggestive
of *The Sound and the Fury*. A girl is defiled by mud and other
filth thrown by "outraged" "friends" and, in a related incident, she stands in the shelter of her lover's (bridegroom's)
arm. In *Absalom, Absalom!*, this time, the actors are not
Judith and Henry but their parents, and the imagery is divided between two scenes in Quentin's experience.

The defilement of the bride and groom after the Sutpen
wedding—mud and rotten vegetables are flung at them—
must have recalled to Quentin his own ruckus with Caddy
when Caddy found him in the barn hugging his playmate,

Natalie. Quentin had plunged into the hog wallow when Caddy told him she didn't "give a damn" what he and Natalie did:

> You dont you dont I'll make you I'll make you give a damn. She hit my hands away I smeared mud on her with the other hand I couldn't feel the wet smacking of her hand I wiped mud from my legs smeared it on her wet hard turning body hearing her fingers going into my face but I couldn't feel it even when the rain began to taste sweet on my lips . . . . (*SF*, 170)
>
>   * * * * *
>
> We lay in the wet grass panting the rain like cold shot on my back. Do you care now do you do you. (*SF*, 171)

The picture of Thomas Sutpen shielding his bride and her aunt "with his body" and "the bride shrinking into the shelter of his arm" (*AA*, 57)—described by Mr. Compson as his father had described it for him—would have reminded Quentin of Caddy's rendezvous with Dalton Ames, the figures of his sister and her lover silhouetted against the darkening sky in the rain. The memory would have been only a month or so old, and it had marked for Quentin the end of honor and the end of the world:

> we reached the fence she crawled through I crawled through when I rose from stooping he was coming out of the trees into the grey toward us coming toward us tall and flat and still even moving like he was still she went to him
>
> this is Quentin Im wet Im wet all over you dont have to if you dont want to
>
> their shadows one shadow her head rose it was above his on the sky higher their two heads
>
> you dont have to if you dont want to
>
> then not two heads the darkness smelled of rain of damp grass and leaves the grey light drizzling like rain the honeysuckle com-

ing up in damp waves I could see her face a blur against his
shoulder he held her in one arm like she was no bigger than a
child he extended his hand
    glad to know you
    we shook hands then we stood there her shadow high against
his shoulder one shadow (*SF*, 191–92)

Mr. Compson brings this chapter to a close at the same
point at which Miss Rosa closed the first chapter, and at the
same time he metaphorically reinforces the rain imagery of
the rendezvous scene—and this in a spell of dry weather (the
drought and dust are so much a part of the September night
that four months later Quentin can "taste the dust" (*AA*, 362)
as he tells his roommate about it). The very people who had
spoiled the wedding, says Mr. Compson, would later

> ". . . be driving out to Sutpen's Hundred to call and (the men) to
> hunt his game and eat his food again and on occasion gathering at
> night in his stable while he matched two of his wild negroes
> against one another as men match game cocks or perhaps even
> entered the ring himself. It blew away, though not out of mem-
> ory. He did not forget that night, even though Ellen, I think, did,
> since she washed it out of her remembering with tears. Yes, she
> was weeping again now; it did, indeed, rain on that marriage."
> (*AA*, 58)

The next two chapters, III and IV, continue Mr. Compson's
narration. Both chapters end with Wash Jones's arrival at
Rosa's house in town after the murder of Charles Bon by
Henry Sutpen. Jason Compson's long talk about Sutpen and
Judith and Henry almost duplicates his talk with Quentin in
The Sound and the Fury. The two conversations are less than
a month apart, so that in the second one Mr. Compson's ob-
servations on incest and suicide, though he speaks only of

Controlling Images in *Absalom, Absalom!*

Judith and Henry, carry ironic weight. They are consciously aimed at Quentin's own problems by a loving father who wants to help and comfort but scarcely knows how. Jason Compson surely knew that his remarks about the overclose relationship between Judith and Henry must be excruciating to Quentin; but he must also have known Quentin's need to wrestle with his problems—through someone else's story if he could not overcome them in first person.

The end-of-the-chapter image is so powerful in the third chapter that it is only hinted at there and is fully developed at the end of the fourth chapter. It is the image of a young man about to shoot his sister's lover (fiance) in the name of honor. The potential victim is an army veteran newly returned from war, a glamorous figure, threatening somehow because of his sophistication and his virility, almost as attractive to his murderer as to the boy's sister. A pistol lies still-unaimed between the two young men.

Mr. Compson cannot imagine why Henry killed Charles Bon, and he gropes for the answer among the images that are almost as real to him as they are to Quentin. For Quentin, though, the message of the images is disastrously plain. His father imagines

> ". . . the ultimatum discharged before the gate to which the two of them must have ridden side by side almost, the one calm and undeviating; perhaps unresisting even, the fatalist to the last; and the other remorseless with implacable and unalterable grief and despair—" (It seemed to Quentin that he could actually see them, facing one another on the two gaunt horses, two men, young, not yet breathed over long enough to be old but with old eyes, with unkempt hair and faces gaunt and weathered as if cast by some spartan and even niggard hand from bronze, in worn and patched gray weathered now to the color of dead leaves, the one with the

tarnished braid of an officer, the other plain of cuff, the pistol lying yet across the saddle bow unaimed, the two faces calm, the voices not even raised: *Dont you pass the shadow of this post, this branch, Charles; and I am going to pass it, Henry . . . ." (AA, 132–33)*

His father's characterization of Henry Sutpen as "remorseless with unalterable grief and despair" launches the parenthetical shift to Quentin's imagination. Remorselessness and unalterable grief and despair are qualities Quentin had felt under similar circumstances a month earlier. The scene then was the confrontation of Quentin and Dalton Ames. For the gate of Sutpen's Hundred there had been a rural wooden bridge near the Compson house, and the unaimed pistol had lain on the bridge railing rather than across a saddle bow. It was Dalton Ames's own pistol and had been offered confidently, for Ames knew Quentin was not man enough to use it. The horses, too, were involved with Quentin's memory of his failure and humiliation: Ames's horse was tethered nearby, and after Ames rode away Caddy arrived on the horse Quentin had left behind to prevent Caddy's knowing where he would meet Dalton Ames. Quentin's quarrel with Ames was identical with Henry's quarrel with Charles Bon: Bon's union with Henry's sister, like Caddy's liaison with Dalton Ames, was by her brother's standards dishonorable. And, more humiliating still, in both cases the younger man was jealous of both his sister and her lover.

The confrontation of Quentin and Dalton Ames is related in *The Sound and the Fury* as Quentin relives it during his fist fight with Gerald Bland on June 2, 1910, the day of Quentin's suicide. (SF, 196–201) It is the climax of Quentin's section of the earlier novel.

There are thirty-nine pages in Chapter V of *Absalom, Absalom!* Less than a page, at the end, is in Roman type. All the rest, italicized, is Rosa Coldfield's bitterly impassioned account of her life at Sutpen's Hundred from the day of Charles Bon's murder until her move back to Jefferson after Sutpen insulted her, and finally of her reaction to the news that Sutpen himself had been killed. " *'Dead? I cried. Dead? You lie; you're not dead; heaven cannot, and hell dare not, have you!'* But Quentin was not listening, because there was also something which he too could not pass—." (*AA*, 172) Here the reader's attention is whipped back thirty-seven pages to the picture past which Quentin has not moved. Rosa's whole diatribe is wiped out.

When she lost Quentin's attention, Rosa had been telling her own imagined version of Henry Sutpen's confrontation with Judith after he had shot Charles Bon. (Of all the characters in *Absalom, Absalom!* only Clytie could have witnessed this scene, but all the narrators create vivid "memories" of it.) Judith and Clytie, as Rosa reconstructs the event, are in an upstairs bedroom sewing on Judith's wedding dress. They hear a shot, then running footsteps on the stair. The door bursts open and Henry stands in the doorway: *"and then the two of them, the two accursed children on whom the first blow of their devil's heritage had but that moment fallen, looking at one another across the up-raised and unfinished wedding dress."* (*AA*, 135)

Taking his cue from this, Quentin has been privately elaborating the vision while Rosa raves on to the empty air, for he and Caddy have had more than one confrontation and, dear as they are to each other, more than one fight. Furthermore, although he failed to kill Dalton Ames, Quentin had wished

desperately to kill him and could have killed him. Quentin's
mud fight with Caddy, when he was fourteen and she twelve,
is evoked here almost more vividly than their differences of
will at the time of the Dalton Ames problem, as is their child-
ish splashing in the brook on the day of their grandmother's
funeral. Another time, about the time of the mud fight,
Quentin had slapped Caddy for letting a boy kiss her:

> *What did you let him for kiss kiss*
> *I didn't let him I made him watching me getting mad What do*
> *you think of that? Red print of my hand coming through her face*
> *like turning a light on under your hand her eyes going bright.*
> (AA, 166)

On the afternoon of their grandmother's funeral, when
Quentin was only seven and Caddy five, he had slapped her
for taking off her dress to dry it. Benjy's memory of it makes
the parallel to Henry's confrontation with Judith even more
apparent, for Caddy stands there in her underwear:

> "You just take your dress off." Quentin said. Caddy took her dress
> off and threw it on the bank. Then she didn't have on anything
> but her bodice and drawers, and Quentin slapped her and she
> slipped and fell down in the water. When she got up she began to
> splash water on Quentin, and Quentin splashed water on Caddy.
> Some of it splashed on Versh and me and Versh picked me up
> and put me on the bank. (SF, 20–21)

In *Absalom, Absalom!* now, in Quentin's mind, the slaps are
verbal, and the imagined words of brother and sister proclaim
the elimination of the lover-rival, Bon-Ames (for Quentin has
already—at the end of Chapter IV—identified Charles Bon
with Dalton Ames):

> But Quentin was not listening, because there was also something
> which he too could not pass—that door, the running feet on the

stairs beyond it almost a continuation of the faint shot, the two
women, the negress and the white girl in her underthings . . .
pausing, looking at the door, the yellowed creamy mass of in-
tricate satin and lace spread carefully on the bed and then caught
swiftly up by the white girl and held before her as the door
crashed in and the brother stood there, hatless, with his shaggy
bayonet-trimmed hair, his gaunt worn unshaven face, his patched
and faded gray tunic, the pistol still hanging against his flank: the
two of them, brother and sister, curiously alike as if the difference
in sex had merely sharpened the common blood to a terrific, an
almost unbearable, similarity, speaking to one another in short
brief staccato sentences like slaps, as if they stood breast to breast
striking one another in turn neither making any attempt to guard
against the blows.
  Now you cant marry him.
  Why cant I marry him?
  Because he's dead.
  Dead?
  Yes. I killed him.
  He (Quentin) couldn't pass that. He was not even listening to
her: he said, "Ma'am? What's that? What did you say?" (*AA*, 172)

Now, at the end of Chapter V, Quentin has all the mental
pictures for which he, with Shreve's help and insistence, will
provide narrative transitions in the following chapters of *Absalom, Absalom!* There is one more controlling image for him,
however; it is presented to him not in "the telling" but in the
flesh. It is his confrontation with Henry Sutpen in the old
house at Sutpen's Hundred, and what it is to control has already happened in *The Sound and the Fury*—Quentin's suicide. Chronologically, Quentin faces the aged Henry Sutpen
on the September night which is the time of the first five
chapters of *Absalom, Absalom!*, but the reader has to wait
until the end of the novel for a description of that sight.

There, in the last chapter, the reader for the first time is offered something like an adequate explanation of Quentin's immobility and his obvious depression during the long night of telling with Shreve at Harvard in January 1910: that since September Quentin has not been free of the sight of Henry Sutpen among the yellow sheets and pillowcases of his deathbed, and that he feels he will never be free of it.

Chapter V, Rosa's long-winded paean to love, honor, and indignation, is the keystone of *Absalom, Absalom!*, although Quentin, we are told, was not listening to most of it. Rosa, a poet, knows exactly how imagery functions in art and in memory. Images, odors, says Rosa in what could be a psychoanalytical study of her young non-listener, are the means of memory: "Once there was—," Rosa begins, and interrupts her own fairytale opening with

> Do you mark how the wistaria, sun-impacted on this wall here, distills and penetrates this room as though (light impeded) by secret and attritive progress from mote to mote of obscurity's myriad components? That is the substance of remembering— sense, sight, smell: the muscles with which we see and hear and feel—not mind, not thought: there is no such thing as memory: the brain recalls just what the muscles grope for: no more, no less: and its resultant sum is usually incorrect and false and worthy only of the name of dream.—See how the sleeping outflung hand, touching the bedside candle, remembers pain, springs back and free while mind and brain sleep on and only make of this adjacent heat some trashy myth of reality's escape: or that same sleeping hand, transformed by that same sleeping brain and mind into that same figment-stuff warped out of all experience. Ay, grief goes, fades: we know that—but ask the tear ducts if they have forgotten how to weep. Once there was (they cannot have told you this either) a summer of wistaria. It was a pervading everywhere of wistaria (I was fourteen then) . . . (AA, 143–44)

The answer to Rosa is, Yes, indeed, Quentin *has* noticed the wistaria sun-impacted on the wall and the dust motes "of obscurity's myriad components." Furthermore, September 1909 is the close of his own "summer of wistaria." He noticed the wistaria-shaped light and shade on page one, as did the reader. And his father has told him that grief fades, even grief like his grief for Caddy's virtue.

At the beginning of the next chapter, Quentin takes over as narrator. Shreve does most of the talking for a while, but at the beginning he only rewords what Quentin has told or is telling him. Meanwhile, the reader, having ascended the picture blocks to Rosa's aesthetic keystone, begins the return to *terra firma* through the narrative blocks of the book's last chapters.

The objective narrator gets the telling started for Quentin and Shreve with the delivery, by Shreve, of Mr. Compson's letter about Miss Rosa's burial. It is the occasion for Shreve to ask his roommate, as he has done frequently since September, to "tell about the South." Moving around to Quentin's point of view but Shreve's words, the reader is given yet another look at Quentin's *vision fixe* from Chapter V:

> the sister facing him across the wedding dress which she was not to use, not even to finish, the two of them slashing at one another with twelve or fourteen words and most of these the same words repeated two or three times so that when you boiled it down they did it with eight or ten. (*AA*, 174)

It is not primarily Sutpen's story that Quentin and Shreve construct. With him they have little in common. The two young men at Harvard are enthralled by Sutpen's children, their own contemporaries in age, and they fall naturally and without competition into the roles best suited to each. There is more than a little role sharing and exchange, but for the most part it is Shreve-Charles and Quentin-Henry.

As the story they are telling moves toward its climax, the death of Charles Bon, Shreve exclaims from time to time, "Jesus, think of his heart!" But Shreve cannot realize the torment through which he is driving his friend, for he is unaware, as far as the reader of *Absalom, Absalom!* can tell, of the girl who takes Judith's role in Quentin's mind—Caddy. "Jesus," Shreve ought to be saying, "think of Quentin's heart!"

The Shreve-Quentin narration, then, begins with the pictured confrontation of Judith with her brother. Although it returns to some of the scenes already discussed as evocative of *The Sound and the Fury,* and although there are evocations (for the reader) of that part of *The Sound and the Fury* which follows Quentin's show-down with Dalton Ames, they are not so appalling, for in January 1910 Quentin has yet to learn of Caddy's engagement, to attend her wedding after learning of her pregnancy, and finally to determine on his own death. The parallels are there, but they are meaningful only to the reader of both novels, not to Quentin.

The end of the telling in Chapter VI introduces Jim Bond, the Negro idiot grandson of Charles Bon. Shreve is rehearsing what Quentin has been telling him of his (Quentin's) first sight of the "hulking slack-mouthed saddle-colored boy a few years older and bigger than" Quentin when Quentin was a child, who lived with Clytie at the decaying Sutpen mansion. Although Jim Bond's howling has orchestrated the burning of Sutpen's house and the immolation in it of Clytie and Henry, just as Benjy's howling has accompanied Caddy's fall from virtue and is to disrupt her wedding, Shreve seems as unaware of Quentin's idiot little brother as he is of Quentin's lovely sister.

Throughout the last chapters of *Absalom, Absalom!*, the dormitory sequence, the narrator continues his practice of taking over for the last paragraph or so of each chapter, and again the effect is to pull the reader away from the Sutpen story, this time not necessarily toward *The Sound and the Fury* but to the "present"—January 1910. It pulls him away from the motion of Quentin's and Shreve's narrative to Quentin's immobility at his desk in the cold room. It fixes this portrait of Quentin in the reader's mind as firmly as the various Sutpen tableaux have been fixed in Quentin's mind, and it is repeated at the ends of Chapters VII and VIII, each of the chapters being pulled back to the scene of the telling, the dormitory room at Harvard.

Chapters VI and VII are largely Shreve's replay, with embellishment, of information he has received from Quentin. Although technically the narration of Chapter VIII is in the "outside" voice of the objective narrator, Quentin and Shreve tussle verbally to do the telling. They become more and more excited as the story runs away with them, and the three-chapter fabrication, "the two of them creating between them, out of the ragtag and bob-ends of old tales and talking, people who perhaps had never existed at all anywhere," (*AA*, 303) arrives, at its climax, right back at the gates of Sutpen's Hundred.

Henry has seen his father in Virginia and has been told (so goes the roommates' narrative) that Bon must not be allowed to marry Judith because (for the first time in the novel) Bon has Negro blood. Bon, confronted by Henry with this information, seems to see it as subterfuge on Sutpen's part. *"He*

did not have to do this, Henry," he declares. "He didn't need
to tell you I am a nigger to stop me. He could have stopped
me without that, Henry." (AA, 356) Bon has given Henry his
coat and wrapped himself in a blanket. As they argue,

> his hand vanishes beneath the blanket and reappears, holding his
> pistol by the barrel, the butt extended toward Henry.
> —Then do it now, he says.
> Henry looks at the pistol; now he is not only panting, he is
> trembling; when he speaks now his voice is not even the exhala-
> tion, it is the suffused and suffocating inbreath itself:
> —You are my brother.
> —No, I'm not. I'm the nigger that's going to sleep with your sis-
> ter. Unless you stop me, Henry.
> Suddenly Henry grasps the pistol, jerks it free of Bon's hand
> and stands so; again Bon can see the whites of his inrolled eyes
> while he sits on the log and watches Henry with that faint expres-
> sion about the eyes and mouth which might be smiling.
> —Do it now, Henry, he says.
> Henry whirls; in the same motion he hurls the pistol from him
> and stoops again, gripping Bon by both shoulders, panting . . . .
> (AA, 357–58)

This scene, powerfully suggestive of Dalton Ames and
Quentin at the bridge in *The Sound and the Fury*, is followed
immediately by Shreve's rapid recapitulation of the murder
and the events immediately following:

> ". . . right up to the gate; side by side and it only then that one
> of them ever rode ahead or dropped behind and that only then
> Henry spurred ahead and turned his horse to face Bon and took
> out the pistol; and Judith and Clytie heard the shot, and maybe
> Wash Jones was hanging around somewhere in the back yard and
> so he was there to help Clytie and Judith carry him into the house
> and lay him on the bed, and Wash went to town to tell the Aunt
> Rosa and the Aunt Rosa comes boiling out that afternoon and

finds Judith standing without a tear before the closed door, hold-
ing the metal case she had given him with her picture in it but
that didn't have her picture in it now. . . ." (*AA*, 358)

Shreve here experiences an epiphany: Bon, though now he is
for Shreve "the black son of a bitch," would have changed the
picture for that of his octoroon mistress so that, if Judith
should have to find a picture on his dead body, it would be
the one that would neutralize her grief.

The refrain of Chapter VIII is virtually the same as the end
of Chapter VII: " 'Come on,' Shreve said, 'Let's get out of this
refrigerator and go to bed.' " (*AA*, 359) It is as spell-shattering
but more effectively functional than Marlowe's "Pass the bot-
tle" in *Heart of Darkness.*

In the last chapter of *Absalom, Absalom!* the objective narrator tells a haunted house story, the story of Quentin and
Rosa Coldfield going out to the crumbling mansion far from
town looking for and finding Henry Sutpen, who has come
home four years earlier and is still there waiting for death.

Quentin and Shreve have at last gone to bed. They lie in
the dark before the opened window and talk about the South,
incidentally unfolding for the reader, more fully than at any
earlier point, the story of that night in September when
Quentin came face to face with his shade, Henry Sutpen—the
boy—now an old man—who had had the strength of will to
kill a man for the honor of his sister and his family. The controlling image again is in Quentin's mind, but it is not the
product of his imagination.

The experience itself, the finding of Henry Sutpen, had had
the quality of nightmare, the illusion of experience repeated
endlessly, a kind of compounded or impacted *déjà vu*—both
for Quentin and for Rosa. There had been Clytie blocking

Rosa's passage up the stair, just as she had blocked it on the day of Bon's murder, for instance, and there had been the closed door at the end of the upstairs hall. Rosa had pressed on and had entered the room behind the door. Terrified, she had rushed down and out of the house. Compulsively, Quentin had approached the room himself, engaged in a brief and circular conversation with the "ghost" and hurried away knowing the experience would be with him always. This confrontation was similar to some of his other confrontations—with Caddy, with Dalton Ames—but there was an allegorical or symbolic significance to this one: Quentin has looked his Doppelgänger in the face, and he has understood that this portends his own death.

Back in his own room, having hastily seen Rosa home, Quentin finds himself soaked in sweat on his bed,

> . . . waking or sleeping he walked down that upper hall between the scaling walls and beneath the cracked ceiling, toward the faint light which fell outward from the last door and paused there, saying 'No. No' and then 'Only I must. I have to' and went in, entered the bare, stale room whose shutters were closed too, where a second lamp burned dimly on a crude table; waking or sleeping it was the same: the bed, the yellow sheets and pillow, the wasted yellow face with closed, almost transparent eyelids on the pillow, the wasted hands crossed on the breast as if he were already a corpse; waking or sleeping it was the same and would be the same forever as long as he lived:
> *And you are—?*
> *Henry Sutpen.*
> *And you have been here—?*
> *Four years.*
> *And you came home—?*
> *To die. Yes.*
> *To die?*

> *Yes, to die.*
> *And you have been here—?*
> *Four years.*
> *And you are—?*
> *Henry Sutpen.* (AA, 373)

Although he goes on answering Shreve's questions, Quentin is saying to himself "Nevermore of peace. Nevermore of peace. NevermoreNevermoreNevermore." (AA, 373) Quentin is "older at twenty than a lot of people who have died" (AA, 377) and he will be dead before he is twenty-one.

VII

The Plot Line:
Manipulation of Sequence in *Absalom, Absalom!*

Narrative skill is essentially the mastery of sequence. The historical chronology of events to be related is almost beside the point. The chronology of the listener's or reader's learning is what makes or destroys a story.

A reader invited into a story *in medias res* finds himself a participant in the telling; he butts in from time to time like Shreve, supplying the names to match the pronouns, demanding "But what about . . .?" and "Do you mean that . . .?," and the narrator must then stop the historical or fictional sequence and back up to reword something or add to it. The "born and bred story teller" operates on this understanding whether speaking face to face with his audience or writing for it.

The twentieth-century fascination with time and relativity, with psychology, and especially, in literature, with the wash and flow of mental activity at various levels of consciousness has obscured for theorists if not for practical craftsmen the unarguable fact that as long as a tale must be transmitted in words or in a series of pictures the telling is linear.

The linear method of narrative might seem not quite appropriate for a writer whose understanding of Time matched that of Henri Bergson; and Faulkner, like Proust and Joyce, Virginia Woolf and—well, nearly everyone writing from the late nineteenth century to the mid-twentieth, tried to combine sequence and duration. His distinction among novelists of *durée* is his recognition that intriguing as *durée* may be intellectually, it has not primacy over the linguistic medium by which it must be imparted: the story is more important than its own content simply because it is prerequisite to expression of that content. This is an old-fashioned tenet, perhaps, but it was instinctive to Faulkner, and it has a down-to-earth practicality which cannot be easily denied: no story (plot), no content, and the story is told one word at a time.

Although he cannot work the whole canvas simultaneously, a writer like Faulkner can and does create the illusion of doing so, though as a teller of tales he deals not in "is" but in "seems" and his medium is linear. His delight is in the manipulation of his reader's belief, and he does it by manipulating the sequence in which he surrenders information, by "playing the line" for all it is worth. The basic skill of a natural born raconteur is this mastery of line, of sequence. The writer is not, after all, a painter.

The most important device by which a writer manipulates chronology is repetition. Once over lightly he tells his tale, then again over lightly, adding a piece of information either omitted in the first telling or teasingly anticipated there, and then a third time, again adding a piece of information—or telling the same thing from another point of view, which has the effect of adding information. It is the pattern of the ghost story ("and then they heard it again, a little nearer") and of the fairy tale in which three wishes are successively squandered or three suitors fail, each in a slightly different way, to win the hand of the princess. The "modern" variant uses distortion of time to accommodate informational sequence.

Bruce F. Kawin, in *Telling It Again and Again*,[1] makes the point that familiarity bred in an audience by repetition is present even in the first telling, because the first telling embodies the writer's memory of the scene as he conceived it and went over it once or several times before he put it on paper, so that it is, on paper, a kind of ritual reenactment—and this is tacitly understood between writer and reader.

Kawin is interested not only in written fiction, which is dependent on language even for its "pictures," but in film, where pictured movement depends upon repetition of the photographic image from frame to frame with only slight positional changes of an arm or an eyelid to create the phenomenon of "the moving picture." In his book, Kawin explores the aesthetic and psychological functions of repetition—visual repetition, verbal repetition, and experiential repetition (memory). It is not surprising that in his consideration of repetition in novels he devotes much space to Proust's *A la recherche du temps perdu*, a novel Faulkner told Löic Bouvard that he would like to have written,[2] and to *Absalom, Absalom!*, or that he writes a great deal about Bergson and refers frequently to Dr. Lawrence Kubie's *Neurotic Distortion of the Creative Process*.[3]

---

[1] Bruce F. Kawin, *Telling It Again and Again: Repetition in Literature and Film* (Ithaca and London: Cornell University Press, 1972).

[2] Loic Bouvard, "Notes and Discussion: Conversation with William Faulkner," tr. Henry Dan Piper, *Modern Fiction Studies*, 5 (Winter 1959–60). Originally in *Bulletin de l'association amicale universitaire France-Amerique* (January 1954), 23–29. Reprinted in *Lion in the Garden: Interviews with William Faulkner, 1926–1962*, eds. James B. Meriwether and Michael Millgate (Random House, 1968).

[3] Laurence S. Kubie, M.D., *Neurotic Distortion of the Creative Process* (Farrar, Straus and Cudahy, 1961). Originally c. 1958, 1961 by the University of Kansas Press.

Dr. Kubie distinguishes between creative activity and its aberration in terms of repetition: artistic or creative repetition exhibiting progression by means of slight variation from instance to instance; neurotic repetition being exact, fixed, compulsive. Both creative and neurotic repetition, thus understood, are easily demonstrated by Faulkner's young protagonist, Quentin Compson, who is both artist and suicide.

Quentin's presence in *Absalom, Absalom!* is the choice of Miss Rosa Coldfield because she knows Quentin to be interested in the history of his town and county (Mr. Compson speculates that it is also because Rosa suspects Quentin may already know some of her and Sutpen's family secrets). But Quentin's performance in the tasks of chronicler reveals Faulkner's reasons for using him in the novel and reveals him to be in *Absalom, Absalom!* the very same Quentin who went to pieces in *The Sound and the Fury* over Caddy's loss of honor and his own loss of Caddy. Even in the last half of *Absalom, Absalom!*, when Quentin seems to be as carried away as Shreve is with the excitement of creative narration, the objective narrator describes him again and again as stuck, motionless, frozen, on one of the confrontation images evoked by the tale they tell. There he hangs while the narration flows past him, forward, under the control of his roommate. Of course, both the forward movement and Quentin's inability to move are under the control of the ultimate narrator, William Faulkner, and Quentin's mental and emotional condition is an important element of Faulkner's plot.

Repetition in narrative brings the reader or listener back to a point passed or arrived at earlier, and his recognition of that point makes him feel that he stands again on a spot where he has stood before, indeed that he has remained there for some time. For the reader, then, the interval during which he read thirty-six pages (as in Chapter V of *Absalom, Absalom!*) is as if it had not happened. Obviously, it has happened, and the reader is not fooled—maybe exasperated, but not fooled. However, he has already willingly suspended disbelief and invested of his own time, and he is likely to permit himself almost deliberately to fall into a further misconception—that the novel is getting nowhere and that he is himself outside or beyond time.

While Faulkner's notions of Time are characteristically twentieth century, all *durèe* and relativity, his narrative technique is less contemporary. As suggested earlier, and as most Faulkner scholars agree, it is in the oral tradition of nineteenth-century American southern and western story-telling. Faulkner's cohorts in narrative technique are Mark Twain and the anonymous frontier tall tale tellers. They include also Ambrose Bierce, who, in the last sentence of "An Occurrence at Owl Creek Bridge," by snapping his hero's neck in a hangman's noose, denies the fact of the man's escape, which he has just narrated in detail. Faulkner's plot lines are also similar to those of Edgar Allan Poe, who would have been proud to have written "A Rose for Emily," and who withholds until the end of "The Fall of the House of Usher" [4] information which belongs before the narrator's

---

[4] Richard P. Adams has compared *Absalom, Absalom!* and "The Fall of the House of Usher" in detail. See "The Apprenticeship of William Faulkner," *Tulane Studies in English*, XII (1962), 113–56. Reprinted in *Faulkner: 4 Decades of Criticism*, ed. Linda Welshimer Wagner (Michigan State University Press, 1973). Adams fails to note, however, Faulkner's significant use in *Absalom, Absalom!* of two words on which Poe virtually held the patent—*ratiocination* and *Nevermore*.

realization of it—the information that Roderick Usher, having entombed his "dead" sister, was beset by the realization that she had only appeared to die, that he had sealed her living in the family crypt. Finally, released from her coffin and the crypt by the elemental violence which rends the crumbling foundations of the House of Usher, she stands before her brother in her shroud—a scene remarkably like the one Quentin imagines in *Absalom, Absalom!* where Judith Sutpen snatches up her wedding dress to confront Henry across it, or the scene in *The Sound and the Fury* where Caddy in her negligee, a shroud as far as Quentin is concerned, tells him "I've got to marry someone." (*SF*, 142–43)

The narrative return to a given point in the plot is sometimes called looping. Some manifestations of it are called flashback, especially in cinema. Occasionally an academic or "intellectual" novelist, for example John Fowles in *The French Lieutenant's Woman*,[5] flaunts the device *as* a device, along with his authorial privilege, even at the expense of deliberately insulting his trusting (gullible) reader.

Novels, or sets of novels—what might be called multinovels—in which the same characters and events are described in overlapping sequence by several narrators, or from several points of view, are designed on this principle of return to a given point in time and space, the effect being, generally, the renunciation of calendar and clock, the feeling that time has been declared null and void.

This is not the same manhandling of time that occurs in circular plots, where stories swallow their own tails like the Midgaard serpent—for instance, *Finnegans Wake*. In looping

[5] John Fowles, *The French Lieutenant's Woman* (Boston and Toronto: Little, Brown and Company, 1969).

plots, beneath all the backward movements there is a forward progression which takes the reader, if not along the shortest distance between two points, at least along a convoluted scenic route. Good examples, outside Faulkner, are the two trilogies of Joyce Cary, Ford Madox Ford's tetralogy *Parade's End,* and Lawrence Durrell's *Alexandria Quartet,* all products of the twentieth century.[6] Although the entire Yoknapatawpha fiction is a vast multi-novel, only the Snopes trilogy makes a neat enough unit to have been identified as a series within the greater body of Yoknapatawpha fiction, but I think it can be claimed that *The Sound and the Fury* and *Absalom, Absalom!* constitute a multi-novel or dual-novel. Together or singly, these two works made good use of the devices of the multi-novel: repetition, distortion of sequence, multiple point of view, and, in spite of these, forward progression, with *Absalom, Absalom!* wedged into the sequence of *The Sound and the Fury,* though published seven years later.

In *Absalom, Absalom!* the major fresh starts, or fresh attacks upon the Sutpen narrative, are at the beginnings of chapters and each utilizes either a change of narrator or a fresh approach by a "same" narrator. In the last part of the novel, after Quentin and Shreve have been allowed to settle down to serious story-telling, the shift is signalled by a little ritualized exchange between the roommates. It is narrated by

[6] Cary's trilogy of art includes *Herself Surprised* (1941), *To Be a Pilgrim* (1942), and *The Horse's Mouth* (1944). His trilogy of politics includes *Prisoner of Grace* (1952), *Except the Lord* (1953), and *Not Honour More* (1955).

Ford's tetralogy, published in 1950 as *Parade's End,* includes *Some Do Not* (1924), *No More Parades* (1925), *A Man Could Stand Up* (1926), and *The Last Post* (1928).

Durrell's *Alexandria Quartet* includes *Justine* (1957), *Balthazar* (1958), *Mountolive* (1958), and *Clea* (1960).

the outside impersonal narrator, and the pattern is this: Shreve, breaking into the stylized Faulknerian "voice" in which he and Quentin collaborate and in which they can hardly be distinguished from one another or from Quentin's father, demands information or affirmation of his own insight. Quentin answers Yes or No, and little or nothing else. Then Shreve responds with a curt, irrelevant, or irreverent burst implying that his patience with the idiot South has about run out.

These mini-exchanges, punctuated in a way that hands them over to the objective narrator, effectively package the content of *Absalom, Absalom!* into chapter-size units, and since they adhere so rigidly to a pattern and occasionally are almost exact repetitions, they function as refrains function in old English and Scottish ballads.

A similar pattern is followed in the earlier chapters, where Quentin is a listener rather than a narrator: either the principal narrator of the chapter (Miss Rosa or Mr. Compson) or the objective narrator abruptly pulls the narrative down to earth at a point anticipating the close of the next chapter or repeating the close of the preceding one, or reaching out toward both.

Once in the "listening" chapters and once in the "telling" chapters the end wording of adjacent chapters is almost identical. At the end of Chapter III Quentin's father tells of Wash Jones's riding Sutpen's "remaining mule" in to town to find Rosa Coldfield and take her to Sutpen's Hundred:

> . . . a gaunt gangling man malaria-ridden with pale eyes and a face that might have been any age between twenty-five and sixty, sitting on the saddleless mule in the street before the gate, shouting "Hello, Hello," at intervals until she came to the door;

whereupon he lowered his voice somewhat, though not much. "Air you Rosie Coldfield?" he said. (*AA*, 87)

In the next chapter Mr. Compson reveals that Jones went for Rosa on the day Henry and Charles Bon returned from the war, and at the end of the chapter he replays the scene before Rosa's house, extending Jones's speech just enough to include the startling explanation of his errand:

> ". . . and then Wash Jones sitting that saddleless mule before Miss Rosa's gate, shouting her name into the sunny and peaceful quiet of the street, saying, "Air you Rosie Coldfield? Then you better come on out yon. Henry has done shot that durn French feller. Kilt him dead as a beef." (*AA*, 133)

In these chapters Quentin is learning. In Chapters VI and VII, where he is telling, the device of almost exactly repeated wording is used again: at the end of Chapter VI, which has looped back to the end of Chapter V where Rosa Coldfield told Quentin that there is "something living in [Sutpen's house]. Hidden in it. It has been out there for four years, living hidden in that house," (*AA*, 172) Shreve finds it all nearly unbelievable. He recounts briefly what he has heard and demands to be told whether he understands correctly:

> "And yet this old gal, this Aunt Rosa, told you that some one was hiding out there and you said it was Clytie or Jim Bond and she said No . . . and so you went out there . . . and you found Clytie and Jim Bond both in it and you said You see? and she (the Aunt Rosa) still said No and so you went on: and there was?"
> "Yes."
> "Wait then," Shreve said. "For God's sake wait." (*AA*, 216)

Chapter VII, next, contains Quentin's rendering to Shreve of the story of Thomas Sutpen's last-born child and the old man's death, almost exactly as Faulkner wrote it in the short story "Wash." At the end of the chapter Shreve again cannot

believe what he has heard, or doubts that he has heard it correctly. His "Will you wait?" reaches back to the close of
Chapter VI and his response to Quentin's answer will be
repeated at the end of Chapter VIII. Here is the close of
Chapter VII:

> "*Will you wait?*" Shreve said. "—that with the son he went to
> all that trouble to get lying right there behind him in the cabin,
> he would have to taunt the grandfather into killing first him and
> then the child too?"
> "—What?" Quentin said. "It wasn't a son. It was a girl."
> "Oh," Shreve said. "—Come on. Let's get out of this damn
> icebox and go to bed." (AA, 292)

By the end of the following chapter (VIII), Quentin and
Shreve have traced Henry Sutpen and Charles Bon through
the Civil War, walking forward through time and backward
with the retreating army through space, and back to the gate
of Sutpen's Hundred. Once more Rosa has been summoned
from town, and once more Judith has found on her fiance's
body the locket containing the wrong portrait. Shreve claims
Bon must have exchanged the pictures to ease Judith's grief:

> "It was because he said to himself, 'If Henry dont mean what
> he said [that he would kill Bon], it will be all right; I can take it
> out and destroy it. But if he does mean what he said, it will be the
> only way I will have to say to her, I was no good; do not grieve for
> me.' Ain't that right? By God, aint it?"
> "Yes," Quentin said.
> "Come on," Shreve said. "Let's get out of this refrigerator and
> go to bed." (AA, 359)

After each chapter ends thus with its refrain, and the plot
comes back down to earth, a new chapter, a fresh start, is possible. Each new chapter begins calmly with a brief indication
of its setting in the "present," its principal narrator, and the

dominant point of view (Quentin's except in the structurally pivotal fifth and the final chapters—and these two chapters are brought around to his point of view at their climaxes). Then the reader follows Quentin into the never-never land (or perhaps to poor Quentin ever-ever land) of Henry and Judith and Charles Bon, to the chapter-ending refrain.

While the Sutpen material contained between the opening and close of each chapter does not follow a straightforward chronology from the start to the finish of the book, it is chronological within each chapter, and the stories and episodes of which it is composed present an artistically graceful swinging to and fro, in arcs of varying length, during the years from 1807 (the birth of Thomas Sutpen) to the close of 1909 (the deaths of Henry Sutpen and Clytie and Miss Rosa). Critics have devoted much effort to establishing what happened when in the Sutpen story, forgetting that some of it is not known to have happened at all, and that it is supposed, anyway, to be sloshing about in Bergsonian duration not in "the annals of time" but in the mind of Quentin Compson. Meanwhile, the *telling* of the Sutpen story moves straight and steady through two short time spans, as indicated by the chapter beginnings.

The first span covers half a day in early September 1909, from about two o'clock in the afternoon until about two o'clock in the morning. The second span covers a somewhat shorter period in mid-January 1910, from sometime after dinner until a few minutes after one o'clock in the morning. During the first span Quentin learns about, or reviews what he has "always" known about, Sutpen and his family; during the second span he and Shreve carry the story forward toward the very recent past, almost to what is for them the present.

Manipulation of Sequence in *Absalom, Absalom!*

Chapters I, II, III, and IV constitute the first time span, with Chapter V being devoted to a rather specialized kind of narration by Miss Rosa combined with her wildly poetic statement about love, the function of memory, and similar abstractions. The refrain of Chapter V, after several rehearsals, puts at the strategically located end of this keystone chapter: Henry Sutpen facing his sister Judith to tell her that he has killed her fiance. As Quentin "sees" it, their exchange is repetitious but brief in a kind of ragged spread-winged butterfly pattern similar to Quentin's exchange with Henry Sutpen at the end of the novel:

> *Now you cant marry him.*
> *Why cant I marry him?*
> *Because he's dead.*
> *Dead?*
> *Yes, I killed him.*

Then Rosa, in the refrain, tells Quentin that "something" has been hidden in the old Sutpen house for the past four years. (*AA*, 172) Its discovery will be the purpose of their trip to the house.

Here are the chapter openings by which Rosa's and Mr. Compson's narrations of Sutpen material are timed:

Chapter I.

   From a little after two oclock until almost sundown of the long still hot weary dead September afternoon (*AA*, 7) . . . the dry September afternoon (*AA*, 10) . . . the dry dusty heat of early September . . . (*AA*, 31)

Chapter II.

   It was a summer of wistaria. The twilight was full of it and of the smell of his father's cigar, as they sat on the front gallery after supper . . . (*AA*, 31)

125

Chapter III is a continuation of Mr. Compson's narrative, but Quentin, who speaks the opening lines of the chapter, reestablishes the setting, and his remark implies that the talk is continuous.

> If he threw Miss Rosa over, I wouldn't think she would want to tell anybody about it *Quentin said.*
> Ah Mr. Compson said again After Mr. Coldfield died in '64 . . . [and he goes on with the narrative] (*AA*, 59)

> Chapter IV.
> It was still not dark enough for Quentin to start, . . . even now the only alteration toward darkness was in the soft and fuller random of the fireflies below the gallery (*AA*, 89)

Chapter V could almost be the mind of Rosa Coldfield while she waits for Quentin, knowing that while he is away from her he and his father will have been talking about her. Nearly the whole chapter is printed in italics, and it is hard to tell when Rosa's private thoughts blur over into her talk with Quentin, but at the end of the chapter it is evident she has been talking for, though Quentin is not listening, he is thinking about something Rosa has said. The chapter opens, "*So they will have told you doubtless already . . .*" (*AA*, 134) The setting is not provided until later in the chapter. Still Rosa is speaking:

> Once there was—Do you mark how the wistaria, sun-impacted on this wall here, distills and penetrates this room . . .? (*AA*, 143)

Here Faulkner has brought the Sutpen legend up to the present. The reader is ready to be told "what" is hidden in Sutpen's house, but the narrative pattern of this first half of the novel will be traced a second time before he will be told.

Again the body of each chapter is devoted to narrative, but from now on it will be consciously contrived narrative. Quentin and Shreve are committed to ratiocination, from the clues provided by tradition and hearsay, of a "truth" with enough explanations in it to satisfy themselves and the novel's readers. But again the process of narrative is steady and straightforward through time, as shown in the openings of the successive chapters. Chapter VI begins:

> There was snow on Shreve's overcoat sleeve, his ungloved blond square hand red and raw with cold, vanishing. Then on the table before Quentin, lying on the open text book beneath the lamp, the white oblong of envelope, the familiar blurred mechanical *Jefferson Jan 10 1910 Miss* and then, open, the *My dear son* in his father's sloped fine hand out of that dead dusty summer where he had prepared for Harvard so that his father's hand could lie on a strange lamplit table in Cambridge: that dead summer twilight—the wistaria, the cigar-smell, the fireflies—attenuated up from Mississippi and into this strange room, across this strange iron New England snow:
> *My dear son,*
> *Miss Rosa Coldfield was buried yesterday.* (AA, 173)

At the end of Chapter V, the past had come up to the present. Now as the narrative pattern begins its second course, Mr. Compson's letter has suddenly turned the present (January 1910) into the past (September 1909), and Quentin begins his narrative for Shreve with his trip out to Sutpen's Hundred with Rosa Coldfield. By the beginning of Chapter VII,

> There was no snow on Shreve's arm now, no sleeve on his arm at all now: only the smooth cupid-fleshed forearm and hand coming back into the lamp and taking a pipe from the empty coffee can. . . . So it is zero outside, Quentin thought; soon he will raise the window and do deep-breathing in it. . . . But he had not done so yet, and now the moment, the thought, was an hour

past and the pipe lay smoked out and overturned and cold. (*AA*, 217)

Chapter VIII:
There would be no deep breathing tonight. The window would remain closed above the frozen and empty quad beyond which the windows in the opposite wall were, with two or three exceptions, already dark; soon the chimes would ring for midnight, the notes melodious and tranquil, faint and clear as glass in the fierce (it had quit snowing) still air. (*AA*, 293)

By these means *Absalom, Absalom!*, like the frog escaping from the well, moves two hops up and slides back one, a process which eventually carries the frog out of the well, brings the novel "to the point," and releases Quentin from his obligations to preserve the Sutpen legend and to explain the South to outsiders. But it does not free him from his self-confrontation, and for this reason he will have "Nevermore of peace."

Between Chapters VIII and IX, Shreve has prevailed upon his frozen Southern friend to leave the "icebox" of their sitting room. The last chapter of the novel (IX) begins: "At first, in bed in the dark, it seemed colder than ever. . . ." (*AA*, 360) The roommates have completed their long fictional narrative, and the author brings the last half of the novel into symmetrical balance with the first half. The symmetry is completed in Chapter IX.

As Chapter V rounded off the listening chapters of *Absalom, Absalom!*, Chapter IX, the last one, rounds off Quentin's contribution to the Sutpen saga. Like Chapter V, too, it contains a good deal of dramatic irony—comment by the author on the narrative process itself.

Chapter IX's vivid dramatization of Quentin's emotional

128

distress, his motionless disquiet followed by chills and shaking, constitutes the objective narrator's longest sustained narrative in the novel. It reveals what the Sutpen fiction has meant to Quentin at this turbulent time of his life and how it has, in fact, been shaped by Quentin's preoccupations. The narrative of this chapter thereby proclaims the importance of Faulkner's having chosen Quentin to be the medium through which the Sutpen story reaches the reader.

The chapter is used, first of all, to relate what transpired at Sutpen's Hundred in September 1909, and second, the immediate impact of that incident on Rosa and on Quentin. Then, while Shreve rattles on, enthusiastically missing the point about as wildly as Boon Hogganbeck missing a treeful of squirrels, Quentin lies unspeaking, impaled on another point of the narrative—the burning of the Sutpen house with Henry and Clytie in it—just as he sat unheeding through Miss Rosa's eloquence in Chapter V.

Quentin has told Shreve about the night at Sutpen's Hundred, and surely Shreve would not have let him omit the identity of the "something" they found there, but the narrator tells us it is to himself that Quentin goes over and over the words he and Henry Sutpen exchanged. The pattern is similar to the exchange he had imagined between Henry and Judith in Chapter V, a little longer perhaps but not much, and, like the other dialogue, bilaterally symmetrical and inconclusive. It ends as it began:

And you are—?
Henry Sutpen. (AA, 373)

A narrative moves—in spite of whatever looping occurs between its beginning on page one and its conclusion on the last page—along a one-way route, for it is accomplished by language. A sentence also moves from its beginning forward through its predicate, usually to an object, direct or indirect. As the novel may have any number of subplots and diversions, so the sentence may carry any number of dependent or independent clauses, and the sentence itself may be compound or complex.

William Van O'Connor has declared that for Faulkner the ideal sentence would be booklength.[7] I think this is unjust to Faulkner's fine sense of plotting and of structure in the novel, but examination of *Absalom, Absalom!* as if it were one long sentence should establish once and for all whether its subject is Quentin Compson, or "the South," or Thomas Sutpen with or without his heirs.

Parsing *Absalom, Absalom!* as a booklength sentence, an analyst might reasonably look for the subject at or near the beginning. There he will find Quentin Compson before he finds Sutpen, and when Sutpen does appear it is as Quentin almost literally sees him during Rosa Coldfield's introductory harangue on *her* subject: "Out of quiet thunderclap he would abrupt (man-horse-demon). . . . Immobile, bearded and hand palm-lifted the horseman sat. . . . Then in the long unamaze Quentin seemed to watch. . . ." (*AA*, 8) Then Quentin's situation is made clear. As Rosa talks and Quentin "seem(s) to watch" the establishment of Sutpen's domain, his

> . . . hearing would reconcile and he would seem to listen to two separate Quentins now—the Quentin Compson preparing for Harvard in the South, the deep South dead since 1865 and peo-

---

[7] "Rhetoric in Southern Writing: Faulkner," *The Georgia Review*, XII (Spring 1958), 83–86. Reprinted in *William Faulkner: A Collection of Criticism*, ed. Dean Morgan Schmitter (New York: McGraw-Hill, 1973), 55.

pled with garrulous outraged baffled ghosts which had refused to
lie still even longer than most had, telling him about old ghost-
times; and the Quentin Compson who was still too young to de-
serve yet to be a ghost, but nevertheless having to be one for all
that, since he was born and bred in the deep South the same as
she was—the two separate Quentins now talking to one another in
the long silence of notpeople, in notlanguage, like this: *It seems
that this demon—his name was Sutpen. . . . (AA, 9)*

This is the subject of the long *Absalom, Absalom!* sentence—Quentin Compson—the double Quentin Compson—
confronting the dead past of the South at a time when he is
about to begin his adult life in the North, the South being
put before him just when he should be putting it behind him.

Faulkner's reputation for verbal profuseness and de-
viousness has effectively preserved a misconception fostered
by first readings of this novel. The intriguing blanks in the Sutpen story, meant to intrigue Quentin, have over the years in-
trigued outsiders (Canadian Shreve, non-Southern critics—
and most of the Southern ones, too) so thoroughly that they
have lost sight of Quentin, and like Quentin they have read
into the novel "facts" and "chronology" and "motivation"
which are missing from it and are meant to be missing.

Quentin is right at the front of the book, at the top of the
first page, and his point of view is quickly established as the
reader looks with him at the sun and shadow on the closed
window blind and at little old Miss Rosa in the too-tall chair
opposite Quentin with her hands on the chairarms "like a
crucified child." (AA, 7) Quentin's presence is important on
the last page, too, and it is he who speaks the overly insistent
last words of the novel, "I don't hate [the South]!"

The claim made here, that Quentin begins and ends the

novel and is primarily the subject of it, is not meant as denial that *Absalom, Absalom!* is *also*, though to a lesser extent, about Sutpen and the South—the South so fascinating to the Canadian Shreve and to Yankee and European critics and reviewers. It is rather to say that without Quentin the reader could not approach either, and that in quest of Sutpen the reader comes much closer to Quentin than he will ever come to Sutpen or the South. As a matter of fact, both Sutpen and the South are, as Quentin tries to tell Shreve, beyond the reach or comprehension of anyone, even of the Southerner, Quentin himself, who (the reader knows) desperately and for entirely personal reasons desires to know the truth about them.

The object of the booklength sentence of *Absalom, Absalom!*, judging by its position at the end of the novel, is the impact on Quentin of his confrontation with Henry Sutpen. The confrontation itself occurred at least four months before Quentin tells Shreve about it and half a novel (the second half) before Faulkner allows the reader to hear of it. Belatedly revealed, the confrontation explains Quentin's emotional disturbance, which has been evident but not explainable up to this point. The position of the explanation—at the end of the plot line—demonstrates the importance to the novel of Quentin's meeting with Henry Sutpen. The meeting is *not* important to anyone's understanding of the South or of Thomas Sutpen—or even of Henry.

The action between this subject and object is not much action, any more than the total number of hours actually covered by the novel is any strain on the classic unity of a twenty-four-hour day. The action of *Absalom, Absalom!*, performed primarily by Quentin, is foreshadowed deftly and at just the right point in the novel's exposition, in the paragraph where Quentin is presented as the subject of the novel. The action consists, first, of Quentin's receiving from Miss Rosa Coldfield and from his father a good deal of information, most of it hearsay, about the long dead Thomas Sutpen and several members of his family and then, in the second half of the novel, of Quentin's sharing the story with Shreve and collaborating with him in creatively filling the gaps in the story.

Although the roommates narrate almost as a single intelligence, Quentin is unable to bring his Canadian friend even close to understanding the South or the people who live there; yet by reliving his own meeting with Henry Sutpen, he intensifies the distress he has felt since that meeting, sharpening the thorn on which he has been impaled since September.

To some extent Quentin's dilemma is his own ambivalent feeling about the South. This ambivalence is implicit in Quentin's protesting too much:

> "I dont hate it," Quentin said, quickly, at once, immediately; "I dont hate it," he said. *I dont hate it* he thought, panting in the cold air, the iron New England dark; *I dont. I dont! I dont hate it! I dont hate it!* (AA, 378)

To a far greater extent, in terms of what is known about Quentin and can be seen behind and beyond *Absalom, Absalom!*, his problem is that he cannot find any appropriate attitude he can assume toward his sister. In effect, the direct object of the sentence of which Quentin is the subject is his realization that for him, as for Sutpen, there is no answer. Quentin is doomed, and the reader who knows *The Sound and the Fury* does not have to be reminded that Quentin will be the instrument of his own death. Indeed, the reader of

only *Absalom, Absalom!* may feel this without fully understanding why Quentin's confrontation with Henry, old and
dying, has lingered so oppressively with Quentin for four
months, literally immobilizing him by January 1910.

The action, again, of *Absalom, Absalom!*—the verb in the
booklength sentence, the novel's plot or movement—is Quentin's *gathering* of information, *assimilating* it, *telling* it, *developing* part of it with Shreve's collaboration, into an elaborate
fictional narrative, and *bringing* his (Quentin's) personal involvement in the tale to such a pitch that the memory of
Henry Sutpen on his deathbed sends Quentin into a fit of
chills in which he can only deny and deny that—almost a non
sequitur—he hates the South.

The Sutpen stories, a body of tales told by a collection of
raconteurs, from Sutpen himself to Shreve McCannon, and
the themes developed by the various points of view, will have
to be incorporated into the booklength sentence as dependent
clauses and qualifying phrases. To break out of the "sentence"
metaphor, they can be mood music or the canvas and pigment
with which the ordeal of Quentin Compson is represented—
or the mirror in which Quentin sees himself and out of which
Caddy will run in April—"her train caught up over her arm
she ran out of the mirror like a cloud, her veil swirling in long
glints her heels brittle and fast . . . ." (*SF*, 100)

It might be argued, I suppose, that it is the other way
around and Quentin is the means of telling Sutpen's story or
"explaining" the post-Civil War South, but that argument
would have first to overcome Quentin's demonstrated position
as subject of the booklength sentence, on one hand, and the
lack of evidence for many of the "facts" Quentin and Shreve
surmise about Rosa's demon or Grandfather Compson's giant,
on the other.

Manipulation of Sequence in *Absalom, Absalom!*

The Sutpen material in *Absalom, Absalom!* is *im*material—literally. It is inadequate for even short fictional units, with the exception of the story of Sutpen's death, and possibly the architect hunt with its exposition of the origin of Sutpen's design. This was made plain to Faulkner by the rejection of "Evangeline." His acceptance of the verdict is evident in his having submitted the story only twice, and then using it as a kind of tool in another, longer and more complex, fiction. When after the publication of *Absalom, Absalom!* the Sutpen material was once again tried out without Quentin, in the stillborn movie script "Revolt in the Earth," it was so flimsy its reader diplomatically refused to acknowledge that Faulkner had had any responsibility for it.

The Sutpen story is not a story at all. There are too many holes in it and no possible access to factual filler for the holes. At best, it is a series of dramatically potent pictures, irresistible to imaginations born and bred to spin yarns—Quentin Compson, William Faulkner, and (after short acquaintance with these two) "outsiders"—Shreve McCannon, readers, critics.

What Faulkner has demonstrated in *Absalom, Absalom!* is the process of fiction and the impossibility of accurate historical reconstruction. The novel is about the creation of a story, a novel, if you will, from "the ragtag and bob-ends of old tales and talking." For Quentin the generative scene is the one at the end of the short first chapter of *Absalom, Absalom!* in which he first identifies himself and Caddy as Henry and Judith Sutpen; but the pivotal, compelling, hypnotic scene, for him, hits closer home, for when *Absalom, Absalom!* begins in September he has just been through it for Caddy in August.

This scene, the murder of Charles Bon, is not withheld either from Quentin or from the reader. It is mentioned early in the novel as part of the Sutpen legend that Quentin has known always, "a part of his twenty years' heritage of breathing the same air [as Rosa] and hearing his father talk about the man Sutpen" and "the son who widowed the daughter who had not yet been a bride." (AA, 11) However, since it is not withheld, and since it has already happened and is widely known to have happened, it can hardly be considered the climax of the novel. Furthermore, since the supposed double motivation—threatened incest and miscegenation—is created out of thin air by Quentin Compson two generations later and has never occurred even in imagination to Rosa (so far as we can tell) or to Grandfather Compson or to Quentin's father, who are all closer to Sutpen than Quentin is, the "revelation" of Henry's motive can hardly be counted except as the highpoint in Quentin's creation of a story mingling ghost figures from the unknowable past with his own experience.

What is withheld until the end of the novel is the scene which is important to the foreground story of *Absalom, Absalom!*: Quentin's meeting with Henry Sutpen. This scene initiates the biggest and most important loop in the plot line of Quentin's involvement in the Sutpen story. It occurs in the center of the book, but the plot line is broken off clean before the incident can be narrated. The line begins again several months later, moves along at compelling speed through Quentin's and Shreve's narrative, and in the last short chapter is swung strongly back and spliced at the broken point. The ghost materializes, and by the process of "looping" he stands (lies dying) in September 1909 at the center of the plot, the whole fiction spreading in both directions of time away from his pale but solid figure. At the same time his image, equally real in January 1910 to Quentin's mind's eye and ear, dominates the last scene of the novel, where it will forever hurl Quentin, Henry's self-appointed double, back to the heart of the novel, to the point where fiction became fact, where the word became flesh, where the legendary Henry Sutpen, who killed his friend for love of his sister, materialized in a ghost story before the eyes of his horrified "creator."

VIII
Portrait of the Artist
as a Young Man Doomed

There is not much evidence outside the novel that Faulkner accomplished in *Absalom, Absalom!* what he set out to accomplish or that he realized accurately the extent or nature of his accomplishment there. According to interviews he granted, to a few things he wrote about his experience as a writer, and to evidence in his biography, *Absalom, Absalom!* was not nearly as important to him as *The Sound and the Fury*. That novel, which grew from the image of Caddy in the peartree—"the only thing in literature which would ever move me very much" [1]—was the darling of his heart, as Caddy was ever the favorite child of his imagination.

Faulkner wrote his publisher that he chose Quentin to narrate the Sutpen novel in order to keep overly romantic trappings out of it, but it is Quentin who insists on bringing them in. Shreve's job was to keep Quentin's narrative realistic, but Shreve's improvisations are almost wilder than Quentin's.

[1] William Faulkner in one of four drafts of an introduction for the 1933 edition of *The Sound and the Fury*, unpublished during Faulkner's lifetime, Jill Faulkner Summers Archive. Two versions have been published recently. One is quoted by James E. Meriwether in "Faulkner Lost and Found," *The New York Times Book Review* (November 5, 1972), 6–7; one appears in the *Mississippi Quarterly* (Summer 1973).

About Sutpen Faulkner said "the old man was . . . too big" [2] to have been understood or appreciated by Quentin or his father or Rosa Coldfield, implying that the author shared Grandfather Compson's feeling that Sutpen was larger than life, an epic hero, even a tragic hero in the grand classic mode, but that is not the Thomas Sutpen cut down by Wash Jones's scythe long before the climax of *Absalom, Absalom!* Well before Sutpen vanished from the action of the novel Faulkner had made it plain that Sutpen was a cold, pragmatic, despotic "little" man, almost a caricature of the Scotch-Irish frontiersman who established a short-lived domain in the antebellum South. It was in the littleness of men like Sutpen that the South fell short of the standards of her third and fourth generation idealists—Quentin, Ike McCaslin, William Faulkner.

Rosa Coldfield knew that about Sutpen, and Quentin knew it. Of course, they were informed by William Faulkner, who knew it first. The question is whether Faulkner and Quentin knew they knew it and were saying it in *Absalom, Absalom!* (Rosa had no doubt. "He wasn't even a gentleman!" (*AA*, 14) she fumed, though she too had come through the distance of time to see him as a demon too big for either heaven or hell.)

That Faulkner never talked much about *Absalom, Absalom!*, and that what he did say was misleading, does not prove necessarily that the book was unimportant to him; and the extent to which this novel is a gathering of fragments, some of them only recently discovered, need not categorize *Absalom, Absalom!* as a salvaging-of-scraps kind of commer-

[2] Faulkner, quoted by Joseph L. Blotner and Frederick L. Gwynn in *Faulkner in the University* (Charlottesville: University of Virginia Press, 1959), Reissued (New York: Vintage, 1965), 274.

cial venture. Complaints about it have more often been against its tightness of weave than against structural looseness or fragmentation. The novel is more than adequately held together by the interwoven, almost matted, narration of its primary and secondary narrators, and the whole is strongly unified by one sad young man, Quentin Compson, already committed by an earlier novel to despair and suicide, Faulkner's protagonist and narrator. This tight structure was not casually or accidentally built.

Although Faulkner as critic or analyst of his own novel seems not to have been infallible, within the work itself there is ample indication that the book is deliberately focused on Quentin Compson, specifically the Quentin Compson of *The Sound and the Fury,* and that through Quentin it demonstrates Faulkner's understanding of the art he practiced, the fictive process by which all novels and stories come into existence. *Absalom, Absalom!* contains, in addition to structural evidence of its author's intent, several statements of the process by which a story-teller converts "fact" into "fiction."

It is a rare story or novel that does not include deliberate statement of its theme, however subtly masked or smoothly slipped in. Wherever they exist, such concise statements may be depended on accurately to reveal their authors' conscious intentions. In *Absalom, Absalom!* there is one such statement for each of the narrators. Each narrator, as though each represented a different facet of the author's aesthetic conviction, is permitted a statement in which to articulate his understanding of the forces and processes at work in the creation of the legends of Sutpen. Although most of the narrators think in terms of reclaiming past truth rather than creating new truth from old data, none of their statements concerns Sutpen or the South, and none is purely personal. All concern the narrative and fictive processes and the experiential nature of the data from which these processes begin.

The statement of the unnamed objective narrator, Faulkner himself, is in the novel all right, but its wording was organized first for another outlet. It was meant for the preface of a new edition of *The Sound and the Fury* in 1933. It would have been written well before the edition's publication date, at about the time Faulkner began work on *Absalom, Absalom!* He withheld the preface from publication, perhaps because he did not want it published, more likely because he wanted to use large segments of it verbatim in *Absalom, Absalom!* The preface was not made public until a dozen years after the author's death.

His art, wrote Faulkner, prefacing *The Sound and the Fury*, "is almost the sum total of the Southern artist. It is his breath, blood, flesh, all," but "it is himself that the Southerner writes about, not about his environment." Speaking for Quentin, Rosa, and all his narrator-creations, as well as for himself, Faulkner claimed in the preface that each Southern writer has "taken the artist in him in one hand and his milieu in the other and thrust the one into the other like a clawing and spitting cat into a croker sack. And he writes." Southern artists are not painters or musicians, says Faulkner. Their tradition is oral, and they "need to talk, to tell . . . to try in the simple furious breathing (or writing) span of the individual to draw a savage indictment of the contemporary scene or to escape from it into a makebelieve region of swords and magnolias and mockingbirds which perhaps never existed anywhere." [3]

Although he was writing here about *The Sound and the*

[3] "An Introduction to *The Sound and the Fury*," *Mississippi Quarterly* (Summer 1973), 411–12.

Fury, Faulkner's words about the makebelieve region "which perhaps never existed anywhere" were used again in *Absalom, Absalom!* There they evaluate the Sutpen story as told by Quentin and Shreve. Although Faulkner claims in the preface to have tried in *The Sound and the Fury* "both of the courses . . . to escape . . . and to indict" and feels that "in this book I did both at one time," [4] he was actually to manage the dual performance more cleanly in *Absalom, Absalom!*. The first part of *Absalom, Absalom!* indicts and the second escapes, through Quentin and for nearly half the novel, into the fairyland of magnolias and mockingbirds.

Faulkner's cat-in-the-croker-sack image is a little too lively for the well-mannered Quentin, but the reluctance of the metaphorical cat is no more sincere than Quentin's reluctance to be thrust into the croker sack of Sutpen legends. At the same time Quentin obviously feels the narrative compulsion Faulkner claims for all Southern artists, and as Faulkner says of them, it is himself Quentin tells about, though he tries to tell about Sutpen and (at Shreve's demand) about the South. By extension, it is himself that Faulkner tells about, though he more successfully masks autobiographical elements than most modern writers have been able to do.

Quentin's own despairing credo is to be found in his long "ripple" soliloquy, quoted at the end of my Introduction. It ends, "maybe Father and I are both Shreve, maybe it took Father and me both to make Shreve or Shreve and me both to make Father or maybe Thomas Sutpen to make all of us."

It is the repetitiousness of existence, both in the individual lifetime and from generation to generation, that defeats Quen-

[4] *Ibid.,* 412.

tin: "maybe nothing happens once and is finished," (AA, 261) and "I am older at twenty than a lot of people who have died." (AA, 377)

Judith Sutpen also has her say. Judith's statement of conviction, as despairing as Quentin's, is spoken to Grandmother Compson when Judith brings her Charles Bon's letter "because you make so little impression, you see." For Quentin's ripple figure Judith uses a weaving and braiding metaphor. The individual's life among other individuals, thinks Judith, is "like five or six people all trying to make a rug on the same loom only each one wants to weave his own pattern into the rug; and it cant matter, you know that . . . and yet it must matter because you keep on trying or having to keep on trying and then all of a sudden it's all over and all you have left is a block or stone with scratches on it." Judith's instinct is to preserve by transferring "from one mind to another," in some more or less memorable transaction, evidence that the individual lived at all: "And so maybe if you could go to someone, the stranger the better, and give them something—a scrap of paper—something, anything, it not to mean anything in itself and them not even to read it or keep it, not even bother to throw it away or destroy it, at least it would be something because it would have happened . . . and it would be at least a scratch, something." (AA, 127)

When General Compson's wife jumps to the conclusion that Judith means to kill herself, Judith denies it in words similar to some of Caddy's in The Sound and the Fury: "Because somebody will have to take care of Clytie" (Benjy, Caddy said) "and father, too." Anyway, says Judith, "women dont do that for love. I dont even believe that men do." (AA, 128)

143

In *The Sound and the Fury* Quentin's father told him that people did not commit suicide for lost love. In *Absalom, Absalom!* Judith's views are relayed to Quentin by his father during their long double-edged talk on the Compson gallery.

Mr. Compson's own thematic summation, also spoken on the gallery, is most characteristic of him in its inconclusiveness. Quentin's father is a lawyer, and he looks to evidence for answers, to "facts" as he has had them from his father (also a lawyer) and his mother, to the headstones in the Sutpen graveyard, and to the letter Judith has compared to a headstone.

Although he has a sympathetic nature and has tried to help Quentin toward understanding of himself and others, Mr. Compson cannot imaginatively bridge the gaps in the Sutpen evidence. The best he can offer is "It's just incredible. It just does not explain. Or perhaps that's it: they dont explain and we are not supposed to know." (AA, 100)

Sutpen himself, according to Grandfather Compson, was something of a raconteur, but he was no theorist. He told of his childhood, evidently just to be telling, with a detachment so complete it was as though he spoke not about himself but about someone who meant nothing to him. Later, with his "design" in ruins, Sutpen could not imagine what he had done wrong or had failed to do. He did not understand any design but that of his own ambition. As for imagining his way into any mind other than his own, he could not even begin.

Of all the narrators in *Absalom, Absalom!*, including Quentin, Rosa Coldfield, herself a writer, seems most nearly to speak for Faulkner as she explicates the functions of experience, memory, and imagery. Hers is the longest and the only impassioned statement. Its position in the very middle of the novel underscores its significance.

About remembered reality—the stuff of fiction and poetry and all literature—Rosa says: "That is the substance of remembering—sense, sight, smell: The muscles with which we see and hear and feel—not mind, not thought: there is no such thing as memory: the brain recalls just what the muscles grope for: no more, no less: and its resultant sum is usually incorrect and false and worthy only of the name of dream." (AA, 143)

About our all-too-human self-defensive preference of fancy over fact, she says: "There is that might-have-been which is the single rock we cling to above the maelstrom of unbearable reality." (AA, 149–50) And: "There are some things which happen to us which the intelligence and the senses refuse . . . which stop us dead as though by some impalpable intervention, like a sheet of glass through which we watch all subsequent events transpire as though in a soundless vacuum, and fade, vanish; are gone, leaving us immobile, impotent, helpless; fixed, until we can die." (AA, 151–52)

The quality of Rosa's war poetry is not weighed in *Absalom, Absalom!*, and unlike Vladimir Nabokov who begins his *Pale Fire* with a long narrative poem by one of the characters in that novel, Faulkner provides no examples. The inference of most readers is that it was "only" the output of a dizzy little old lady, but I think Rosa may have been a good poet; hers are the utterances of one who practices the imaginative arts of a professional writer and knows exactly how the creative mind transforms experience into fiction (or poetry) by the evocative use of imagery selected willy-nilly from memory.

"O furious mad old man," sings Rosa Coldfield, poet of The Lost Cause and one-time "androgenous advocate of all polymath love," "I hold no substance that will fit your dream but I can give you airy space and scope for your delirium." Or, in prose: only an imagination like mine can support and preserve a story such as yours.

As for Shreve McCannon, the outsider and the latecomer to the tangling-untangling of the Sutpen yarn, his truly is a charmed performance. Shreve improvises freely and gaily, seeing all too clearly for Quentin's comfort what must have been. Shreve plays the story-telling game with enthusiasm, but, alas for Quentin, it *is* a game for Shreve.

Quentin does not want to resolve the story he has started. He has come up against a brick wall. On its rough surface he reads the hideous scrawl—INCEST—and he hears echoing off it his own unvoiced cry, *Caddy, Caddy,* and his pitiful lie, *Father, I have committed incest.* Although Quentin will not or cannot tell Shreve why he thinks Henry Sutpen killed Charles Bon, he has guided Shreve so far down the narrative path that Shreve utters the unutterable for him—and then claims credit for having thought of it.

It is Shreve who forces the issue of incest in *Absalom, Absalom!* and Shreve who invents Eulalia Bon and her lawyer, but in justifying "his" invention he does give credit where he thinks it is due. He cites Rosa Coldfield as she has instructed Quentin.

When Shreve commands, "And now we're going to talk about love," (AA, 316) and Quentin, immobile at his desk, objects, "But that's not love," Shreve demands, "Because why not? Because listen. What was it the old dame, the Aunt Rosa, told you about how there are some things that just have to be whether they are or not, have to be a damn sight more than some other things that maybe are and it dont matter a damn whether they are or not?" (AA, 322)

Shreve's success as a teller of tales about a land and a people he does not pretend to understand is explainable only by his emotional distance from them. Uninvolved as he is, he is invaluable to the novel's fulfillment. Without his Southern roommate Shreve might never even have wondered much about the South, but without Shreve Quentin would have been able to avoid—for a while at least—confronting the issue which was suffocating him. Without the collaboration of their complementary young minds, Faulkner could not have brought *Absalom, Absalom!* so vividly to life.

The double narrator, or the collaboration of two friends one of whom is the primary narrator, stood Faulkner in good stead more than once, especially in his earlier stories and novels. Tom Dardis concludes the Faulkner section of his book *Some Time in the Sun* with the observation that although William Faulkner, like most of the other novelists who earned their living in Hollywood during the lean 1930s, may have received too little recognition for his efforts at film writing, and he may actually not have earned his salary—from his employers' point of view—the Hollywood method of two or more "writers" talking out a plot until it fell into shape was helpful to him in the writing of his novels. There can hardly be a better example of this than Faulkner's dramatization of it in *Absalom, Absalom!*

Since each of the narrators in that novel, even Shreve, contributed a statement about the nature of experience and of fiction, it is unlikely (impossible) that Faulkner could have failed to appreciate their unifying function. Through them, and especially through Quentin, he was able to hold together a scattering of short stories and to superimpose upon the antebellum schmaltz and vainglory of those stories the frustration Quentin felt in comparing his immediate and personal flesh-and-blood anxiety, an anxiety he could not cope with and wasn't being permitted to cope with if he could have, with the purposeless struggle being forced upon him to relive and to magnify the dead and pointless past.

Furthermore, Quentin's presence in *Absalom, Absalom!* provided Faulkner with the chance to repeat or to approximate the unusual satisfaction—almost a kind of rapture, to hear him tell it—with which he produced *The Sound and the Fury*, an experience he had not expected ever again to know.

Still, when a student asked him in one of his question-and-answer sessions at the University of Virginia whether the Quentin Compson of *Absalom, Absalom!* were the same as the Quentin of *The Sound and the Fury,* he answered simply Yes and did not elaborate. The answer is not as surprising as the student's need to ask the question, but the calm brevity of the reply is. Maybe the student was just trying to provide Faulkner with a topic on which to expound; if so, his effort failed.

Faulkner's portrait of Quentin as a young man, a Southern artist, doomed, did not "just happen" during the compilation of a collection of stories, "the ragtag and bob-ends of old tales and talking." The novel is a portrait of the artist as a young man, and since the young man in the fiction is a suicide, it is also a "sorrows of young Werther." Like James Joyce's famous youthful self-portrait and like Goethe's, *Absalom, Absalom!* traces the artist's growing disillusion with his inherited tradition, his recognition that its heroes are unheroic, its values false, and its demands excessive. Like Stephen Dedalus, young Werther, and all heroes of *Kunstlerromanen*, Quentin—at least in his attitudes—is a but thinly disguised autobiographical figure, and his dilemma of whether to love or to hate, to credit or to denounce, is the dilemma of his creator, the author of the book in which he exists.

Stephen's triple denunciation of family, church, and nation, however, is too coldblooded for Quentin, as its equivalent was too much for Goethe's young Werther. These two suicides, Quentin and Werther, could neither renounce nor admit the renunciation forced upon them. For each of them the several facets of his inherited beautiful but rotten world were focused in the figure of a girl, a sister in one sense or another, who must be surrendered to another; and neither found it possible to live with the required compromise—to admit the loss of innocence and love.

It is worth noting that although Stephen, Werther, and Quentin, the portrayed young artists, differed in their reactions to the problem of impossible choice, all three did renounce and by doing so escaped their problems—simply walked away from them to Paris or to death (any solution is better than none), but their authors did not. For the writers, renunciation by the proxy of their created characters was not only acceptable but preferable.

The career patterns of the three unrelated writers—Joyce, Goethe, and Faulkner—are much alike though they vary in length and in details of content and attitude, and their three portraits of the artist as a young man mark the same turning point in each career. Any writer's self-portrait of a young man similarly sign-posts a turning away from romance and sentiment. Although it is impossible that the change can be complete—once a romantic, always at least trailing clouds of glory—the writer opens his perspective, making room most importantly for humor.

After *Absalom, Absalom!* Faulkner's mockingbirds and magnolias vanish in the dust raised by the ribald stampede of spotted horses. Even the demon ghost of Thomas Sutpen makes way for the clownish advance of Snopses on hamlet, town, and mansion. They had been there all the while waiting in the wings, but they had not enjoyed the spotlight. The protagonists of Faulkner's later novels sometimes wore their creator's mask, as Quentin did, but those subsequent masks were not molded on melancholy youthful features.

Another change made inevitable by the turn away from romance, by the repudiation of hoopskirts and magnolias, is toward simplicity. Although Faulkner continued to employ a very tangled plot line, none of the later novels is as deliberately convoluted as *Absalom, Absalom!* For one thing, none of the other works had such a hodgepodge of stories only ostensibly about one man; and for another, none of Faulkner's later protagonists provided their creator with the resource of irony available to *Absalom, Absalom!* in *The Sound and the Fury.* The serindipitous gap in the earlier account of Quentin's year at Harvard made possible one more all-important appearance for Quentin in the literature of Yoknapatawpha County, and it gave William Faulkner a rare, maybe a unique, opportunity to rewrite and to relive an acknowledged masterpiece, his portrait of a young man doomed.

Written portraits of the young artist are always posthumous. Suicide or not, the young self is remembered by the writing self. A painter's portrait, by contrast, is "from life" though in mirror image. Quentin's death had already been written when he was called upon to sit for his own and Henry Sutpen's and William Faulkner's portrait. Faulkner was already thinking Snopes when Rosa Coldfield thrust Sutpen upon Quentin and told him

> . . . there is little left in the South for a young man. So maybe you will enter the literary profession as so many Southern gentlemen and gentlewomen too are doing now and maybe some day you will remember this and write about it. You will be married then I expect and perhaps your wife will want a new gown or a new chair for the house and you can write this and submit it to the magazines. (*AA*, 9–10)

Index

---

[1] In an early draft (the wistaria paragraph partially quoted opposite the table of contents of this book) Faulkner wrote that, according to Rosa Coldfield, Judith and Clytie "were born at the same hour on the same day in the same dark room."

---

[2] Like Peter's denial of Christ, Quentin's denial of Caddy calls for the atonement of suicide.

Index

---

[3] Faulkner himself wrote Malcolm
Cowley that he tried "to say it all in
one sentence, between one Cap and
one period."